Music
and morals
Dispelling the Myth That Music Is Amoral

Music
and morals
Dispelling the Myth That Music Is Amoral

Kimberly Smith

WINEPRESS WP PUBLISHING

Packaged by WinePress Publishing, PO Box 428, Enumclaw, WA 98022. The views expressed or implied in this work do not necessarily reflect those of WinePress Publishing. The author(s) is ultimately responsible for the design, content, and editorial accuracy of this work.

Unless otherwise noted, all Scriptures are taken from the King James Version of the Bible.

PLEASE NOTE: At the time of publication, the web site addresses referred to in this book were valid; however, due to the unpredictable nature of the internet, no guarantees are made that the information will not change or be removed from the web. We apologize for any inconvenience this may cause.

ISBN 1-57921-765-6
Library of Congress Catalog Card Number: 2004098539

CONTENTS

ACKNOWLEDGEMENTS

Thank you to my family: they have been a real joy and blessing to me, and I value their help with this project. A special thank you to my husband for his patient support. I love you all.

Thanks to music evangelist Alan Ives for enthusiastically sharing some of the material that appears in this book, to Dr. Jim Logan for his encouragement, to Rachel for her proofreading skills, and to Diana for her insights.

Finally, I never could have put this book together so quickly without the prayers of my family and friends. Thank you.

INTRODUCTION

W hat else could you possibly write about music?" my children asked when I told them I needed to write another book. Plenty.

My first two books were received well by those sincerely looking for biblical answers to their concerns about today's contemporary Christian music (CCM), and these people felt I had honestly hit the nail on the head.

Those of the opposing viewpoint were defensive, critical, and even angry. When my husband and I were handing out free copies of my second book, *Let Those Who Have Ears to Hear*, at a certain denominational convention, one pastor actually threw a book back into our box and got, shall we say, huffy.

If these people would do the research I have done, and read the books I have read, hopefully they would reach the same conclusions as I have reached, and reject CCM from its inception. I realize though, that most people are not inclined to do research, especially on a subject about which they don't want to learn the truth (music). After all, they might have to give up their favorite style of music—which was once my favorite style of music, too, until I learned the truth. Let's face it, rock music, Christian or otherwise, has quite an appeal to the flesh.

So that's what this book is all about—compiling the research, quotes, references, and facts about music in an easy-to-read format, complete with a simplified reference guide about different styles of music and their origins.

I hope and pray it will shed much needed light on this very emotional issue of music in general, and contemporary Christian music in particular.

—Kim

SOLI DEO GLORIA

CHAPTER ONE

MUSIC AND MORALS

Have you ever watched one of those old romance movies made in the 1940s, or 1950s, and noticed that when the sweet heroine walks into the room, there's beautiful violin music playing? When her rival, the vixen, enters the scene, however, we hear a sultry jazz saxophone or clarinet announce her presence. My daughter reminded me that cartoons, such as *Bugs Bunny*, also use these same musical cues to give information about the different characters' personalities to their young audience.

Even back then, movie and cartoon makers knew the power of suggestive music to convey a particular message, portray an emotion, or communicate a mood, and today, music is still used in film making to move the story line along and create in the audience whatever feeling or mood the movie makers desire to evoke. Imagine a movie scene with an innocent little girl entering her home. Happy, lilting music in the background would create an entirely different feeling than if that music was eerie and foreboding, wouldn't it?

Picture this: clips of television footage with large, grim-faced football players charging and tackling each other to the background music of a classical ballet. The result is comical, and the music doesn't match the video portion, unless comedy is the intention of the producer. Put this same footage to hard rock music, and the feeling is different, even adrenaline pumping, conveying to the spectators competition and battle.

Why does the meaning of the same video or film sequence change if a different type of music is paired with it? Because music has an effect on us, which is able to manipulate our emotions and thoughts in many ways.

While I am in no way advocating indiscriminate movie viewing, using examples from movie and television music helps us to better understand how music affects us by seeing how it enhances the visual experience, changing our emotions to fit the images we're watching.

Think how flat movies would be if there was no music. Music can and does communicate mood and portray emotions. And composers, filmmakers, and editors can manipulate our emotions through music; yet, most of the time we're not even aware that the music—by design—is changing our mood to the desired effect the filmmaker wants to achieve. A well-placed lone violin or cello playing melancholic music can undoubtedly stimulate our emotions and bring us to tears faster during a sad movie scene than if there was no music at all.

Most of us probably agree that different types of music do cause different emotions or feelings in us, depending on the musical style, yet most of us do not agree that music is moral or immoral. Many people (Christians especially) are under the impression that music is amoral—that it does not mean anything in particular or convey anything morally, other than the message of the lyrics that are put with it.

It stands to reason, however, that if music is so powerful to change our perception and emotions about a given situation, such as the little girl going into her home, then it can also convey sensuality, merely by the planned design of the composers to do so.

Let's return to the first example of the sweet heroine, portrayed by the sweet violin music, and the sultry vixen, portrayed by the sultry jazz saxophone or clarinet. Would it convey the same meaning of innocence if we put the sultry music to the character of the sweet heroine? Not at all.

Why does each type of music perfectly match the character of the movie? Because music does convey morality, and it doesn't need the aid of a movie image to enhance its effect; it can stand alone because it is very powerful. Consequently, music itself is moral or immoral, never amoral.

This morality, or immorality, is determined by specific musical techniques designed and used by composers to musically portray a message apart from lyrics, much like filmmakers choose specific camera angles, lighting, clothing, setting, and, of course, music to help tell the story and get a message across visually and emotionally, rather than simply through dialogue. And just as some movies show immoral images, some music also portrays immorality, simply by the way it is arranged.

When I was in my early teens, a friend and I would listen to a particular album by Herb Alpert and the Tijuana Brass. On that album, there were a couple of pieces that conveyed serious immorality, simply through the techniques used by the band, and all without any lyrics. To be quite blunt, this music was strip-tease music. Would we use this in our churches, put Christian lyrics to it, and call it amoral music? I would hope not.

Music and morals have long been linked in the secular world. Think back to the Roaring Twenties—the era of flappers, prohibition, speakeasies, and jazz music. This period in U.S. history was just after WWI and society was seeking a good time to help forget its previous troubles. Art, literature, and music reflected what was happening in the culture, and people were concerned that morals had greatly declined. Young women began wearing garish makeup and short skirts (for that time), cut their long hair, and danced with full-body contact in frenzied movements to jazz music.

Clearly, the jazz music was a reflection of the Roaring Twenties' attitude of "eat, drink, and be merry," and everyone knew that this music was distinctly associated with loose morals.

The Church during this time, however, did not view jazz music as amoral and adopt it as a form of music ministry so that they could "reach the unchurched," and be "seeker sensitive." The Church had earlier also rejected dance hall music such as the *cancan* with its attendant chorus line of girls entertaining men with high-kicking dance steps. Cancan music was not "redeemed" by putting Christian lyrics to it so that the churches could attract men to be evangelized;[1] in fact, the cancan was considered "naughty."[2]

Until the advent of contemporary Christian music (CCM, a term that includes soft rock praise and worship music) there was a general understanding about the connection between morals and musical styles. Before CCM, hymns were always played "straight," which indicated moral uprightness; traditional church music of generations past did not "swing." And certainly, until the advent of CCM, no drum sets appeared in churches or at revival meetings.

In today's Christian culture, most people rationalize that just about any type of music is acceptable, so long as Christian or moral words are included; however, as we will see, lyrics, by themselves, do not change the meaning of the musical vehicle.

Different musical styles reflect, or convey, different morals and philosophies, and many times there has been a dance, or dance movements, which portrayed those values. We'll see more examples of how morality and music are intertwined throughout this book, as well as look at the decline of music through the ages and how this decline has affected us.

For now, an essential truth for us to understand is this: *The morality of almost any music usually manifests itself in the behavior of those listening to it,* and this is true whether or not there is an "official" dance, which displays the morality of each different type of music, such as the cancan, the Charleston, the waltz, ballet, folk dancing, salsa, tango, or other popular forms of dance we see today.[3]

While this is not a debate about whether or not Christians should dance, we do need to understand and acknowledge the fact that different types of music can cause us to react with different types of body movements—movements which have moral or immoral connotations.

Music has such a powerful effect over our behavior and emotions that we need to look a little closer at the music itself. We need to examine, scientifically as well as experientially, how different types of music make us react, because our actions, not just our emotions or feelings, change with different types of music. And these actions, or behaviors, are one objective indicator of whether the music is moral or immoral.

For example, how do you react when you listen to traditionally played hymns? Do you want to move your hips in a sensually suggestive fashion? Or do you feel like body-slamming, such as in a mosh pit? We don't react these

5

ways at all when we hear a traditional hymn, do we? People usually behave circumspectly to circumspect music.

Yet, what type of music encourages hip-swinging? What type of music goes best with body-slamming or stage-diving? Are these types of music reverent? Do these types of music help purify the soul and encourage spiritual thoughts and moral behavior?

Do we associate Christian rock music and hip-swinging or stage-diving with dear Christian saints and martyrs, such as Corrie ten Boom, David Livingstone, Jim Elliot, or George Muller, whose self-sacrifice and Christian example touched the lives of tens of thousands of people?

Will there be mosh pits around the throne of God in Heaven? Will there be sultry Christian vocals sung by the angels with a jazz saxophone accompaniment?

If music is amoral, as so many pastors, music ministers, and Christians claim, there will be.

NOTE: For our purposes, the term "contemporary Christian music" (CCM) applies to any Christian music that has an accented backbeat (offbeat, weak beat) and imitates secular forms of music, such as swing, jazz, rock, soft rock, gospel rock, rhythm and blues, soul, hip-hop, punk, heavy metal, etc. The term CCM also includes any praise and worship music that contains elements of rock music.

CHAPTER NOTES

1. At this point, discussion usually arises about the Wesley's practice of using barroom tunes or other secular styles of music for hymns, Martin Luther's use of the popular songs of his time, and Isaac Watts' penning "new" music for his era. Upon honest investigation, however, none of these excuses used to defend today's practice of using sensually suggestive music for Christian worship or outreach is valid.

   Dr. John Makujina, in his book, *Measuring the Music*, has done outstanding research in the chapter, "On the History of Ecclesiastical Music and CCM," with lengthy discussions and direct quotes about the musical choices of the Wesley's and Luther, among other notable contributors to Church music throughout the ages. Dr. Makujina imparts some interesting facts about these men, which are summarized below. John Makujina, *Measuring the Music: Another Look at the Contemporary Christian Music Debate,* Second Edition (Willow Street, PA: Old Paths Publications, 2002), 219–265.

   John Wesley was very particular about music and provided editorial oversight to the hymn-poems Charles wrote and set to secular styles and tunes of their day. John understood music's effect on people, and in 1779 wrote a tract, "Thoughts on the Power of Music." He also recorded his observations about music in a journal, which was later published in the multi-volume set of *The Works of John Wesley: Journal and Diaries.* W. Reginald Ward and Richard P. Heitzenrater, eds. (Nashville: Abingdon Press).

   Although Martin Luther was influenced by secular forms of music in his day, he used only one complete tune that was popular in the secular world and played in dance halls and taverns. He changed that tune to an original melody after a few years, yet it reappeared in another hymn after Luther's death (and after its popularity in the secular world subsided). If one reads about Luther and his music, it becomes clear that he, too, was very conscientious about the music he used and understood its power. Additionally, taking a tune or part of a tune and adapting it for another purpose was common at that time, yet we read that Luther avoided the "rollicking drinking songs" of the day.

Isaac Watts' contribution to hymnody was to pen hymn-poems that included lyrics about Christ and His work on the cross for us, a message that had been lacking up to that point, and he published a hymnbook in 1707. His hymn-poems were set to existing tunes already familiar to Christians at that time.

We can see in these examples that each hymn writer/composer was very particular about the music he chose. And if we honestly evaluate the music they selected, we can easily discern that none of it appeals to the flesh in the way that much of today's Christian music does. None of it causes the body to move in a sensually suggestive manner because the morality of the music these men applied to their hymns, whether or not the original lyrics were barroom oriented, was upright as we will see in chapter ten, "How to Discern Moral and Immoral Music."

Measuring the Music: Another Look at the Contemporary Christian Music Debate by John Makujina is available through Old Paths Publications. See the Resource Guide (Appendix Four). Read my first book, *Oh, Be Careful Little Ears*, chapter three, for further information and documentation about hymnody, and pp. 84–86 for a discussion about Martin Luther.

2.   Theodore Baker, ed., "Cancan," *Pocket Manual of Musical Terms*, Fifth Edition, revised by Laura Kuhn (New York: Shirmer Books, 1995), 45.

3.   Of course, depraved man can, and does, pervert anything; however, as a general rule, the morality of most any music will be portrayed by the body's natural reaction to the music.

CHAPTER TWO

NATURE: A MUSICAL CREATION?

In 1761, Benjamin Franklin developed the glass armonica, which is a musical instrument consisting of thirty-seven glass bowls of graduated sizes, approximating the pitches of our musical scale. Each bowl closely fits inside the next, with a horizontal rod inserted through the middle of them all. As a flywheel connecting the rod to a foot treadle rotates the bowls, dampened fingers can play several notes at once. When Ben's wife first heard this instrument in the middle of the night, she thought she was in heaven, hearing angelic music.[1]

If you or your kids have ever successfully produced a tone by running a damp finger around the top of a stemmed glass, you've heard what this sounds like, and you've also successfully demonstrated that music is nothing more than vibrations.

Here's a quick grammar school science refresher: Vibrations are measurable science, and everything we hear is a vibration of an object. Objects, when set in motion, vibrate at different speeds, and these vibrations produce sound waves. *Frequency* is how many sound waves an object produces per second, and when we hear a tone or sound, we are hearing its frequency. The faster something vibrates, the higher the pitch, or note, we hear; the slower something vibrates, the lower the pitch. Of course, there are many frequencies (sounds) above and below the range of our human ability to hear.[2]

When we produce a tone with a glass, as discussed above, we are finding and maintaining the frequency at which the glass vibrates, resulting in a (musical) sound. If a singer can duplicate and sustain this frequency long enough, the glass will crack, or even shatter, because the vibrations get larger and larger.

It's also interesting that for almost any musical sound, the vibration sets up its own harmonic series of tones we are unable to hear. For example, when a violin string is plucked we hear its fundamental sound, which is the beginning of its vibration. Each half of the vibration divides itself into more vibrations, and this process repeats for each subdivided vibration, creating higher pitches (overtones), which are indiscernible to the human ear.

While some of these overtones are not considered musical, the tones that *are* musical make up what is referred to as the harmonic series, on which our western civilization (European) music was based.[3] Of course, composers (many of whom were Christian) during the earlier historical periods of music didn't have access to this science, but they were following this musical law of nature, nonetheless.[4]

Early astronomers and mathematicians have taken this law of harmonics and applied it to science, speculating that because the harmonic series can be explained mathematically and in terms of ratios, most anything having to do with science that can be expressed in numbers and ratios can be placed within the harmonic series, implying that creation is structured according to harmonics.[5] For example, Johannes Kepler, a sixteenth century mathematician and astronomer (and Christian), calculated that the planetary orbits, when expressed in ratios, closely corresponded to musical intervals.

Although today early theories such as this one by Kepler (who helped establish the scientific study of astronomy) have been dismissed by mainstream scientists, they nevertheless provided an important foundation for modern scientific thought and practice.

Yet, in his book, *The World Is Sound: Nada Brahma, Music and the Landscape of Consciousness,* Joachim-Ernst Berendt, German author, broadcaster, and jazz critic, has assembled an amazing amount of information, which explores the idea that science and musical harmonics *are* related. He tells us that a synthesized recording was made of how the positions of the planets would sound if placed as musical notes on a keyboard, according to Kepler's calculations:

> Just as Kepler had computed it, they assigned the contra-G (the low G, situated far to the left end of the normal piano keyboard) to the planet Saturn. On that basis, Kepler's laws define the tones of all other planets, from Saturn to Jupiter, Mars, Earth, and Venus all the way to the one closest to the sun, to Mercury, which is the four-line E sharp, a note that lies almost at the highest end of the piano keyboard.[6]

> The sound spectrum of the six visible planets including Earth covers eight octaves, almost identical with the human hearing range.[7]

Mercury "chirps," Mars "slides up and down" several notes and Jupiter "has a majestic tone reminiscent of a church organ."[8]

NASA has made actual recordings of planetary sounds, which were gathered by various space missions (e.g., Voyagers I and II, Galileo, and Cassini). These planetary "songs" are within the range of human hearing and are similar to sounds such as gongs, choirs, bells, crickets, and wind.[9] These are not sounds from a planetary musical scale or position in space, but from vibrations produced by the interaction of magnetic particles and solar wind (to simplify). The sounds around Earth resemble dolphin clicks, whale songs, and the ocean.

Continuing with Berendt's findings:

> The entire microcosm is replete with harmonic concurrences. The long strings of nucleic acid in DNA are structured precisely according to . . . the fourfold subdivision of the octave (octave, fifth, fourth and major second).[10]

The law of octaves, described by scientist John A. Newlands, was another early idea that seemed to fit into the law of harmonics as it applies to science. Comparable to a tone repeating itself every eighth note (an octave), the periodic table of elements (chemistry) also shows that chemical properties repeat in intervals of eight, with an increasing atomic number.[11] The law of octaves was rejected as the table was further developed, but the repetition of properties is still there. It's also interesting to learn that "all atoms seek to have 8 electrons in their outermost shell."[12]

Further observations explained through the proposed science of harmonics:

The different zones of a crystal can be expressed by numbers that in turn can be translated into notes, since they are of harmonic origin.[13]

. . . some scientists are beginning to regard the atom as a kind of tiny musical note.[14]

The ratios which in music are known as the fifth and fourth intervals occur again and again throughout nature.[15]

The earth's sonic frequency is . . . exactly twenty octaves below the audible range of man. The tone of the atom is twenty octaves above the audible range of man. Therefore, man is placed audibly exactly mid-way between the microcosm and the macrocosm.[16]

These few examples of how science and music seem to relate to one another are intriguing, but I suggest we proceed with caution, because it's easy to jump to conclusions just to prove a point. While we don't want to make any assumptions that aren't there, neither do we want to make the mistake of ignoring God's orderly Hand in the disciplines of science, math, or music. It's obvious that certain numbers and ratios do appear regularly within the realm of science; if they are meant to be placed in the musical harmonic scale remains to be seen. It's a possibility. One thing is certain: God's fingerprint is everywhere we look, as evidenced by the mathematics that apply to both science and music.

There are many people who do believe there is something to this theory of musical harmonics; there are many who do not. I think more research is needed to confirm or discount this theory. Jazz musician and composer Gary Peacock, however, after studying the relationship between music and molecular biology and organ physiology for four years, once commented that, "It becomes clearer and clearer to me that the actual structure of tone in music and the actual structure of matter are the same."[17]

Whether or not creation fits neatly by way of mathematical ratios and formulas into the harmonic series (and, for now, we must all come to our own conclusions), each of us are well aware that music surrounds us in nature, from the cricket's chirp to the whale's song; from the ocean's peaceful rhythm of waves crashing on the beach to the tiniest bird's song.

It's also no surprise that all around us are audible and inaudible vibrations—music—from the tiny atom to the solar system. Even an Australian male spider plays music by plucking the web of his intended to attract her attention.

Perhaps the early scientists and mathematicians of centuries ago were right: perhaps nature *is* structured in musical patterns. In our quest to be "scientific," I wonder if we have dismissed the possibility of God using musical equations in the Divine order of the universe?

Nevertheless, we do know that music is important to God. He created it for our enjoyment and praise of Himself, and it is one of only a few things we experience on Earth that will also be in heaven.

Though the jury is still out about the relationship of science to the musical harmonic scale, modern scientific developments have given us the ability to objectively measure music's moral or immoral effect on our lives, which will be discussed in the following chapters.

Chapter Notes

1. Bryna Stevens, *Ben Franklin's Glass Armonica* (New York: Dell Publishing, 1983 by Carolrhoda Books, Inc.). Frequent glass armonica concerts are given at Colonial Williamsburg by Dean Shostak, owner of one of about fifty glass armonicas in the world. His instrument has forty-two bowls. The music is truly amazing and beautiful. CDs are available through the Colonial Williamsburg Foundation. http://www.colonialwil liamsburg.com, or by contacting Mr. Shostak, who is available for concerts (see Appendix Four for further information).

2. Obviously, this is a simplification of the science of sound.

3. Deryck Cooke, *The Language of Music* (London: Oxford University Press, 1959), 40–41.

    Thomas W. Tunks, "Harmonics." *World Book Online Reference Center*. 2004. World Book, Inc. (Nov. 1, 2004). http://www .worldbookonline.com/wb/Article?id=ar246500.

4. It is thought that Moses and other Old Testament writers also knew about harmonics because they used these same principles in their music, writing in both major and minor keys. Suzanne Haïk-Vantoura, *The Music of the Bible Revealed* (Berkeley, CA: BIBAL Press, 1991), 128-130; 506-509. This is a fascinating book: musical symbols, called *cantillation signs,* occur within the entire Hebrew Bible. Many of these have been deciphered and some of the music has been recorded. Because of the music's continuity in style, Ms. Haïk-Vantoura believed that just as the text was inspired by God, so was the music which was written to accompany the text.

5. Pythagoras; Ptolemy; Johannes Kepler; Johann Bode (Bode's Law); 20th century proponents: Hans Kayser, Rudolf Haase, Joachim-Ernst Berendt. A word of considerable caution: The

Internet is replete with rabbits to chase in this area, many of which contain New Age thinking, mysticism, healing, or other far-reaching and questionable theories and practices.

6. Joachim-Ernst Berendt, *The World Is Sound: Nada Brahma, Music and the Landscape of Consciousness* (Rochester, VT: Destiny Books, 1991; a division of Inner Traditions, Rochester, VT 05767), 66. Willie Ruff and John Rodgers of Yale University produced this recording. NOTE: This book is not written from a biblical worldview; discretion is advised.

For those who are interested in more explanations about Kepler and harmonics as it applies to the planets, here are a couple of interesting web sites:
- http://home22.inet.tele.dk/hightower/spheres.htm. This is a very informative article tracing harmonics from the ancient Greeks to modern science; towards the end it strays into endocrinology.
- http://www.skyscript.co.uk. Caution: This is an astrology web site; however, there is an in-depth article on Kepler's life and work. Click "articles," scroll down to "Johannes Kepler and the Music of the Spheres."

7. Berendt, *The World Is Sound*, 66.

8. Ibid.

9. Center for Neuroacoustic Research, 1988. http://neuroacoustic.com. The NASA recordings were compiled into CDs (for purchase) by Dr. Jeffrey Thompson, an acoustic vibration researcher. Sound clips are available to hear via the web; however, be advised that this web site also promotes music to alter brain waves for meditation and purported healing purposes.

10. Berendt, *The World Is Sound*, 69.

11. Western Oregon University. "A Brief History of the Development of the Periodic Table," 1997. http://www.wou.edu/las/physci/ch412/perhist.htm.

12. DeWitt Steele and Gregory Parker, *Science of the Physical Creation in Christian Perspective,* Second Edition (Pensacola, FL: A Beka Book, 1996), 132.

13. Berendt, *The World Is Sound*, 86.

14. David Tame, *The Secret Power of Music* (Rochester, VT: Destiny Books, 1984; a division of Inner Traditions, Rochester, VT 05767), 219. NOTE: Another fascinating book to be read with caution and discernment.

15. Ibid., 228, referring to the work of Gyorgy Doczi, *The Power of Limits* (Shambhala Publications USA, 1981).

16. J.L. Read, "Creative Harmonics," 1997. http://www.enchantedmind.com/html/science/creative_harmonics.html. NOTE: This web site has interesting articles on science and music; however, some of the information is not from a biblical worldview.

17. Tame, *The Secret Power of Music*, 228.

Chapter Three

How Music Affects the Mind

If we understand and acknowledge the fact that music affects us positively or negatively, if we are aware of music's effect on our lives, we can begin to have true discernment.

How can music affect us? It can affect our mind, our emotions, and our behavior. In this chapter, we'll look at how music affects our mind; that is, our brain, intellect, and mental abilities.

Do you remember how you learned your abc's? You sang a little song, didn't you? It's no secret that setting facts to music can aid learning, and we remember things that are associated with music. Large corporations use this technique to their advantage by creating clever and catchy commercial jingles.

And what about movies, which move a story line along through song? We can remember the song lyrics to these musicals more accurately than we can recall the actual dialogue. Can you finish this phrase: "Super-cali-fragi-listic . . . ."? These types of songs stay with us forever, it seems.

Setting facts to match the rhythm of a musical melody is a proven learning technique; however, the debate over the "Mozart Effect," the idea that simply listening for ten minutes to Mozart's music increases intelligence, continues.

Exciting and promising preliminary findings in the early 1990s reported that after listening to Mozart's *Sonata for Two Pianos in D* (K. 448) subjects scored higher on a spatial/temporal test than subjects who listened to either a tape of relaxation instruction or silence, although the "effect" lasted only for about 10–15 minutes.[1]

This soon spawned popular books and CDs claiming the simplified generalization that listening to Mozart's music would boost IQs and enhance learning. This is not an accurate representation of the facts, and further studies were done that raise more unanswered questions.[2]

Disappointing as this may be, there have been promising studies done with music,[3] and I would argue that listening to Mozart, or any other baroque or classical period composer, would be beneficial for, if nothing else, music appreciation and enjoyment of the music itself—broadening one's horizons and contributing to the proper development of the whole person.

We cannot ignore the evidence that listening to or playing music is essential to our well-being, even if we don't understand why.

But while the science of the "Mozart Effect" has both advocates and critics, the music of Mozart and other contemporaries of his time is timeless, refreshing, and moral.

And it just may be that listening to Mozart's music really does help aid learning and memory; time will tell.

Meanwhile, learning to *play* a musical instrument seems to have the most benefit to the brain, perhaps because during the learning and practicing processes, the brain is working in many areas all at once, which then positively carries over into other areas, such as cognitive and language development, reasoning, creativity, behavior, and more.[4]

For instance, a study reported in the July, 2003, issue of *Neuropsychology* concluded that verbal memory was higher in children who took music lessons for six—or even less—years, compared to children who had no lessons; the longer a child took lessons, the better the results.[5]

The good news is that it's never too late to learn a musical instrument. While it's best to start early to take advantage of the brain's developmental stages, the brain can still change to accommodate any new endeavor, such as musical training, as we age.[6] And music lessons may very well be beneficial to people who have suffered brain injuries.[7]

Early musical training, though, does seem to affect brain size. For example, pianists who began their training before age seven have a larger *corpus callosum*, which is the bundle of nerves that carries information between both hemispheres. It's thought that because the brain must continually coordinate both hands, it creates more connections, but there's no evidence at this time that a larger brain area as a result of learning a musical instrument indicates a higher IQ.[8]

Aside from the debate about using music as a way to raise IQ scores, there are other scientific research studies that show how music does affect the mind positively or negatively.

Positive Effects of Music on the Mind

- Music can alter brain waves. We have four types of brain waves: beta, alpha, theta, and delta. Beta are our normal, alert brainwaves. When we hear quiet, gentle music, or other quiet and soothing sounds, such as the babbling of a brook, more of our brain waves move into the alpha state, which helps us to relax and also lowers our blood pressure, giving us a feeling of well-being.[9]

- Music that contains a tempo between fifty-five to sixty-five beats per minute causes the brain to slow the heartbeat to a healthy rhythm. As a result, blood pressure is lowered and stress factors in the blood are reduced.[10] The slower movements of concerto music written in the baroque period were composed at this tempo. (A beat in this instance is not a drum beat we can hear, but the normal pulse in music to which we would tap our toes.)

- Music that contains high frequencies helps the brain recharge: the higher the frequency, the more the brain is recharged. The best recharging frequencies are between 5,000 hertz and 8,000 hertz, with optimum benefits at 8,000 hertz. Interestingly, the music of Mozart has been found to contain more of these high frequencies than other composers.[11] (Recall from the previous chapter that frequency is the number of times a sound vibrates every second; the more times it vibrates, the higher the pitch. Frequencies are measured in hertz. The notes on the piano range from approximately thirty hertz [the lowest note] to the highest note of about 15,000 hertz. Mozart's music contains more of the moderately higher notes.)

- Music can emotionally reach autistic children.[12] It may also help treat dementia.[13]

- Music may be an effective treatment for some forms of epilepsy. Epileptic seizures were significantly reduced using Mozart's *Sonata for Two Pianos* (K. 448) in a study comparing the benefits of silence, Old Time Pop Music, or the Mozart *Sonata*.[14]

Negative Effects of Music on the Mind

- Music that contains low frequencies, like the noise we hear at airports or construction sites, is considered to be a "brain drain." Rock music falls into this category, because of the bass guitar and other "low pounding sounds."[15]

- Stress and addiction: A driving drum rhythm in excess of three to four beats per second will put the brain into a state of stress, regardless if the listener likes or dislikes the music. And when the brain is in this stressful state, it will release opioids—a group of natural hormones that function like morphine—to help return itself to normal equilibrium and sense of well-being. These natural opioids, if experienced often enough, can be addicting, creating in the listener the continued desire for that "high," somewhat like the high runners experience.[16]

- Another study discovered that when mice were exposed to erratic drum beats similar to those found in "heavy metal" music, their brains tried to compensate by developing a significant number of irregular and pathologically changed neurons.[17] Of course, these are mice, not people, but one has to wonder what effect a continuous exposure to erratic or continual heavy drum beats, such as in some types of rock music, may have on young children's developing brains.

• Certain drum rhythms can cause altered consciousness, which will be discussed further in chapter six.

The brain is a very complex organ, and science is just beginning to scratch the surface of music's effect on the brain. Indeed, we are "fearfully and wonderfully made," and these studies confirm that music is not neutral: it does have an effect on us, whether or not we understand it, and whether or not we want to believe it.

Yet, regardless of any objective scientific studies that man can conduct, God has made us so that the proper use of music refreshes us, lifts our spirits, helps us to cleanse our minds, and energizes us; yet some types of music can make us depressed, stir up wrong emotions, or even cause aggression. We may not understand, scientifically, just why music has the ability to bring about these different states of mind, but most of us have had these experiences. Anecdotal evidence from many people experiencing the same effect often pushes the discipline of science into "how and why."

For the Christian, one who has a personal relationship with the Lord Jesus Christ, science may be important, but it is not as important as our behavior—our attitudes and actions towards ourselves and others, as well as toward God.

With this in mind, the question becomes: Is it moral for us as Christians to use identifiable musical styles and techniques that cause proven negative effects in the brains and lives of our listeners?

Chapter Notes

1. Marilyn Elias, "The 'Mozart Effect' Is Scaled Back a Few Notes," *USA Today* (Aug. 19, 2003). http://www.usatoday.com/life/2003-08-19-mozart_x.htm.

    N. M. Weinberger, "'The Mozart Effect': A Small Part of the Big Picture," *MuSICA Research Notes, 2000,* Volume VII, Issue 1 (Winter 2000). http://www.musica.uci.edu.

    N. M. Weinberger, "Matters of Opinion: 'On the Importance of Being Accurate'," *MuSICA Research Notes, 1998,* Volume V, Issue 2 (Spring 1998). http://www.musica.uci.edu.

2. Ibid.

3. Promising studies:
    - N. M. Weinberger, "Health and Therapies: 'Mozart Enhances Spatial-Temporal Reasoning in a Case of Alzheimer's Disease,'" *MuSICA Research Notes, 1999,* Volume VI, Issue 2 (Spring 1999). http://www.musica.uci.edu.
    - N. M. Weinberger, "The Powers of Music: A Treatment for Epilepsy?" *MuSICA Research Notes, 1998,* Volume V, Issue 3 (Fall 1998). http://www.musica.uci.edu. (*Mozart Sonata for Two Pianos,* K. 448, had the best results.)
    - N. M. Weinberger, "To the Point: 'Music Improves Vocabulary Development,'" *MuSICA Research Notes, 2000,* Volume VII, Issue 3 (Fall 2000). http://www.musica.uci.edu.

4. N. M. Weinberger, "Matters of Opinion: 'Music Research: A Broad View,'" *MuSICA Research Notes, 2000*, Volume VII, Issue 3 (Fall 2000). http://www.musica.uci.edu.

N. M. Weinberger, "'The Mozart Effect': A Small Part of the Big Picture," *MuSICA Research Notes, 2000*, Volume VII, Issue 1 (Winter 2000). http://www.musica.uci.edu.

5. John von Rhein, "Classical Music: 'Music and the Mind,'" *World Book Encyclopedia* (Chicago: World Book, 2004), 126–127.

6. N. M. Weinberger, "Music, Development, Aging, and the Brain: 'It's Never Too Late for Music'," *MuSICA Research Notes, 1996*, Volume III, Issue 1 (Spring 1996). http://www.musica.uci.edu.

7. von Rhein, "Classical Music: 'Music and the Mind,'" 127.

8. N. M. Weinberger, "Brain Anatomy and Music," *MuSICA Research Notes, 1999*, Volume VI, Issue 2 (Spring 1999). http://www.musica.uci.edu.

9. N. M. Weinberger, "Student Music Scientists: 'Physiological Response to Music Stimuli,'" by Jonathan Stocking, *MuSICA Research Notes, 2000*, Volume VII, Issue 2 (Spring 2000). http://www.musica.uci.edu. NOTE: Subjects listened to Mozart's *Piano Sonata #1 in C major* or silence. The alpha waves in the music listeners' brains increased more than those who listened to silence, and there was a "significant decrease in blood pressure in the music group." Reproduced with permission. Dr. Norman M. Weinberger and the Regents of the University of California.

Joshua Leeds, *The Power of Sound: How to Manage Your Personal Soundscape for a Vital, Productive, and Healthy Life*

(Rochester, VT: Healing Arts Press, 2001; a division of Inner Traditions, Rochester, VT 05767), 87; 175-176. NOTE: This is a very interesting book; however, because it delves into areas such as altering consciousness, and creating trance through music or other rhythmic sounds, caution is greatly advised.

10. Sheila Ostrander and Lynn Schroeder, *Superlearning 2000* (New York: Dell Publishing, 1994), 80–81.

11. Ibid., 114. NOTE: They are summarizing decades of research by French researcher, Dr. Alfred Tomatis. I do not endorse, nor recommend, everything promoted by this book or Dr. Tomatis; nevertheless, the science concerning high frequencies refreshing the brain is intriguing.

12. N. M. Weinberger, "To the Point: 'Music "Gets Through" to Autistic Children,'" *MuSICA Research Notes*, *2000*, Volume VII, Issue 2 (Spring 2000). http://www.musica.uci.edu.

13. N. M. Weinberger, "Music Therapy: 'Music Therapy is an Effective Treatment for Dementia,'" *MuSICA Research Notes*, *1999*, Volume VI, Issue 3 (Fall 1999). http://www.musica.uci .edu. This summarizes an article by S. M. Koger, K. Chapin, and M. Brotons (1999). "Is Music Therapy an Effective Intervention for Dementia? A Meta-analytic Review of Literature." *J. Music Therapy*: 36, 2–15.

14. N. M. Weinberger, "The Powers of Music: A Treatment for Epilepsy?" *MuSICA Research Notes*, *1998*, Volume V, Issue 3 (Fall 1998). http://www.musica.uci.edu.

15. Ostrander, *Superlearning 2000*, 114.

16. John Blanchard, *Pop Goes the Gospel*, Revised Edition (England: Evangelical Press, 1991), 187–188. From the study,

"The Neurophysiology of Rock," by Drs. Daniel and Bernadette Skubik. Endorphins are one part of the group of opioids.

17. Gervasia Schreckenberg and Harvey H. Bird, "Neural Plasticity of *Mus Musculus* in Response to Disharmonic Sound," *Bulletin of the New Jersey Academy of Science*, Vol. 32. No. 2 (Fall 1987), 77–86. NOTE: CCM proponents have gone to great lengths to try to discredit these findings; however, Dr. John Makujina has deftly verified and clarified the study's accuracy in his book, *Measuring the Music,* Second Edition (Willow Street, PA: Old Paths Publications, 2002), 201–203.

The experiment is also described in the article, "What's Wrong with Rock," by Louis Torres, 2003. http://www.bibleuniverse.com/rock.asp.

NOTE: The World Wide Web has many resources about music. Type into a search engine "rock music's effect on the brain," or another area you wish to research. A word of caution: There are many claims to music and its effects, benefits, uses, and power. Some of these are New Age or otherwise contrary to biblical Christianity. Be on guard.

The very best resource for accurate and objective music scientific information is MuSICA: The Music and Science Information Computer Archive located at the University of California, Irvine. http://www.musica.uci.edu.

CHAPTER FOUR

HOW MUSIC AFFECTS BEHAVIOR AND EMOTIONS

Vacationing in Florida in the Spring of 2003, our family stopped at a bookstore to browse. My daughter wanted me to listen to a CD of the Chipmunks. Remember Alvin and his brothers singing and talking in their chipmunk voices? We laughed at how funny they sounded. Immediately afterwards, I decided to review the movie soundtrack to *Gods and Generals*. From laughter, I was instantly plunged into a melancholy mood.

Maybe you've had the experience many of us had in our (unsaved) teen years: that of driving fast in our cars while listening to loud and upbeat rock music. The music raised our adrenaline, and we felt energized and carefree as we sped down the highway.

I once did a seminar session in which I began by playing examples of different types of moral music—dramatic, eerie, melancholy, peaceful, funny, and a march. The point was to get the listeners alert to the fact that their moods were changing—that they were being manipulated by the music and were not even aware that this was happening.

Norman M. Weinberger, professor in the Department of Neurobiology and Behavior at the University of California, Irvine, confirms: ". . . music can rapidly and powerfully set moods and do so in a way not as easily attained by other means."[1]

In the last chapter, we saw scientific evidence that music can positively or negatively affect our brains. And because music can positively or negatively affect our brains, or minds, this can result in a changed mood, emotion, or behavior. For example, have you ever purposely listened to godly, moral music or hymns to change wrong thinking or a bad mood? Unless there are serious emotional or psychological problems, this is a very effective way to improve one's state of mind and move thinking in a positive direction.

Music also goes past our reasoning, past our judgment, and directly to our behavior and emotions. It bypasses the intellectual part of the mind, so to speak.

Think about young people's conduct at a rock concert (even Christian rock concerts). In response to the music, there's lewd behavior and sensually suggestive dancing. The concert goers don't actually think to themselves, "I'll move my body sensually." The music simply bypasses their reasoning, and they move in response to the music.

Immoral music seems to act like a cloak, allowing people to excuse their actions; it's a type of covering for sinful or destructive behavior. And not only does the immoral music create a covering for immoral actions, it silently gives permission for people to lose their inhibitions by enveloping them and clouding their judgment. Think about this. Most people don't go around acting out lewd behavior at the office or in the grocery store, but play music with a sensual or heavy beat and watch what happens.

I was at a Christian convention in which there was to be a huge Sunday service. My daughter and I arrived in time to see some of the artists rehearse. As a woman played the piano and sang a bluesy, smoky sounding "Christian" song, a man standing near the sound booth closed his eyes and began to sway sensually to the music, as if in a bar. I seriously doubt that he would have swayed sensually if the music was played straight or in a traditional hymn style. And it's also doubtful that he would have behaved in this manner on the street, without music.

It's as if people are hypnotized by the immoral music. The hypnotic effect of certain rhythms will be discussed more fully in chapter six, but the point is this: Just because Christian lyrics are put to immoral music doesn't change the music's effect on the brain or behavior. It causes people to respond with uninhibited, sensually suggestive movements and other unChrist-like conduct, whether or not they admit it, and whether or not they are aware of it.

We can easily and objectively demonstrate this by contrasting people's behavior at a traditional performance of Handel's "Hallelujah Chorus," from the *Messiah*, to people's behavior at a CCM/P&W concert: there will be a huge difference. The *Messiah* crowd will behave circumspectly, in reverence of the awe-inspiring music. The CCM/P&W concert goers, on the other hand, will be swaying or dancing with sensually suggestive movements to the music. At more extreme CCM concerts, such as a "Christian" metal concert, the attendees will participate in mosh pits, stage-diving, or other destructive behavior.

Why the difference in the crowds? Because, usually, the morality of each type of music will manifest itself in the behavior of those listening to it. Although both of these types of music have words about God or Jesus, the audiences will react primarily to the music, not the lyrics.

It bears repeating: for the most part, the morality of almost any music usually manifests itself in the behavior, or emotions, of those listening to it. Conversely, it is also true that the (momentary or long-term) morality or emotion of a person will also manifest itself in one's choice of music.

For example, rebellious music encourages rebellion, and rebellious people want to hear rebellious music. Do rebellious or troubled teenagers want to listen to traditional hymnody? No. They're drawn to hard-driving, loud, dissonant, aggressive music (usually hard rock, heavy metal, rap, punk, goth, or similar types of music).

What kind of music will a person who is focused on sensuality choose? Sensual music, such as some types of jazz, or other music with a "laid-back," swinging rhythm, because sensual music encourages, or validates, sensuality. What kind of music do we hear in bars and night clubs? Sensual, flesh-appealing immoral music, usually rock or jazz, designed to loosen the listener's inhibitions. And many times, the patrons of these places are looking for someone with whom to have a relationship, if only briefly.

Music affects the mind, which, in turn, affects our behavior; our state of mind will also affect our choice of music. This is why it is so important to exercise self-control and choose music that encourages us morally and spiritually, rather than music that feeds our flesh, negative thinking, or immoral emotions.

We've all had the thought, "I feel like listening to [a type of music]." This is a certain indicator that our mood, or state of mind, affects the music we choose, and that our choice of music mirrors and reinforces our mood, as well. Have you ever felt melancholy and wanted to listen to melancholic music? Maybe you've felt excited about an upcoming event and chosen upbeat music to reinforce the joyful mindset.

These examples clearly indicate that music is not neutral because our moods, which affect our choice of music, are not neutral, and we all make these decisions about different types of music whether or not we are aware of what we are doing.

At this point, some people will argue that they can listen to (immoral) music of their choice and it doesn't affect them; that is, they don't act lewdly or sensually or exhibit destructive behavior. Yet, do we know enough about the mind and how music affects us that we can state without a doubt that it is not affecting us (our minds or behavior) in a way contrary to positive spiritual growth?

I don't think anyone can, and neither does Dr. Weinberger: "Our thinking and our behavior are colored by music, which seems to have direct and unconscious access to the brain substrates of much if not all of our individual lives."[2]

In other words, on a subconscious level, music influences our thinking and behavior more than we realize. This conclusion was reached after reviewing a couple of studies—one with music and art, and the other with music and faces.

The first study matched depressing paintings with sad music, and, not surprisingly, the participants involved considered the paintings to be sad; however, when the same depressing paintings were matched with happy music, the subjects said the paintings were positive. Different, positive paintings matched with happy music were deemed positive, but the same positive paintings were considered sad when sad music was played.

The second study had similar results. For example, after listening to depressing music, subjects judged neutral faces as expressing rejection and sadness more than they judged them to be inviting and happy, even though those emotions were not expressed on the faces.[3]

These findings are important, because they objectively demonstrate that we *are* greatly influenced by music, whether or not we know it.

Not only does science affirm that music affects our thinking and behavior, it also reveals that our bodies correctly identify various emotions conveyed through different types of music.

A study was conducted that measured participant's physiological changes in response to three different moods conveyed by music: happiness, sadness, and fear. There were distinct changes for each mood. Here is the published summary of the findings:

> "Happy" involved largest changes in respiration; "sad" involved greatest changes in heart rate, blood pressure, and skin temperature; "fear" was associated with maximal changes in the rate of blood flow. In other words, the findings favor two facts: first, different genuine emotions can be physiologically defined according to autonomic, bodily functions and second, the emotional reactions produced by music are the "real thing." Thus, *music doesn't simply convey intended emotions that we can recognize, but rather induces genuine emotions in the listener.*[4]
> (Italics added)

I would propose that not only does music have the ability to induce these three emotions of happiness, sadness, and fear, but also the full range of emotions, including that of sensuality, and it's all in how a musical composition is constructed.

Science has already identified two musical techniques, which, combined in different ways, convey certain emotions. These techniques are tempo (speed), and articulation (how musical notes are played: in a quick, disconnected way, which is *staccato*; or, in a smooth, connected manner, which is *legato*.) Combining these two techniques creatively will result in four identifiable emotions: happiness, sadness, anger, and fear.[5]

As musicians will recognize, these are oversimplifications of what we do to skillfully execute a piece of music; however, this does show that specific musical techniques that convey emotion can be scientifically identified.

This has serious ramifications for Christians who propose that music is amoral. Besides being able to objectively witness the actions of people responding to different types of music, we can now scientifically measure music's effect on behavior and emotions. But can we prove, scientifically, that certain types of music, specifically rock music, affect us in a sensual manner? Yes.

The previously mentioned study by Drs. Daniel and Bernadette Skubik (chapter three), which demonstrated that the brain releases opioids in response to the steady drum rhythms in certain types of rock music, also showed that the body releases gonadotrophins (sex hormones), which "enhance sexual arousal."[6] Loud, booming bass music has a similar effect and it's no wonder that adolescent males prefer these types of music: they are either stimulating a release of brain chemicals, stimulating their hormones, or both.[7]

The drums and bass of rock music are not the only way to stimulate sensuality, however. If that were the case, then movies would use rock music to suggest sultriness when the film's siren enters the room. They don't, do they? As discussed in chapter one, sultriness is easily portrayed by a saxophone or clarinet played in a slow, suggestive jazz style, and we don't need a visual image to clarify what we are hearing. If we are all honest, we know what this type of music means. And because this type of music has the ability to portray to us the meaning of sultriness, such music also has the ability to stir up sensual desires in people merely by its musical suggestion; therefore, it's immoral music on both counts: musically portraying sensuality and emotionally stirring up desires.

Emotions are affected by music; this has been scientifically proven. Perhaps that's why we are so reluctant to give up soft rock P&W, CCM, and other types of rock or jazz music—because our emotions have been stimulated, or even manipulated. And just as we are passionate about defending other areas of our lives that have emotional meaning to us, such as our spouse, our children, or our property, we go to great lengths to defend our choice of immoral music—because it touches and influences our emotions. In fact, we may even be emotionally *committed* to our personal music.

This is also a spiritual issue because it is very likely that since emotions are touched, and in the case of opioids being released into the brain an addicting "high" is achieved, people are equating these types of stimulation through music with a spiritual experience.

For the sake of people's spiritual welfare, it's important that we help them differentiate between a musically-induced emotional state, or even an adrenaline rush, and true worship, which is by faith. True worship is not a "feeling" generated by any type of music, either moral or immoral. True worship comes from within our hearts, acknowledging that we are unworthy and prostrating ourselves figuratively, if not physically, before a holy God.

Music has power: It influences our thinking and behavior and not only conveys emotions, it produces genuine emotional states in the body.[8] This power has been speculated about for centuries, even in ancient civilizations, and now, in the last few decades, these speculations have been substantiated by scientific evidence.

Once we understand these facts, we should apply this knowledge in a moral manner, beneficial to the minds, behaviors, and lives of both ourselves and our listeners.

Chapter Notes

1. N. M. Weinberger, "'Elevator Music': More Than It Seems," *MuSICA Research Notes*, *1995*, Volume II, Issue 2 (Fall 1995). Reproduced with permission. Dr. Norman M. Weinberger and the Regents of the University of California. http://www .musica.uci.edu.

2. N. M. Weinberger, "The Coloring of Life: Music and Mood," *MuSICA Research Notes*, *1996*, Volume III, Issue 1 (Spring 1996). Reproduced with permission. Dr. Norman M. Weinberger and the Regents of the University of California. http:// www.musica.uci.edu.

3. Ibid. NOTE: There have been other objective studies done concerning how music affects emotion, thinking, and behavior. Go to The Music and Science Information Computer Archive (MuSICA) at http://www.musica.uci.edu.

4. N. M. Weinberger, "Feel the Music!!" *MuSICA Research Notes*, *2001*, Volume VIII, Issue 1 (Winter 2001). Reproduced with permission. Dr. Norman M. Weinberger and the Regents of the University of California. http://www.musica.uci.edu.

5. Ibid.

6. Blanchard, *Pop Goes the Gospel*, 188.

7. Leeds, *The Power of Sound*, 112.

8. N. M. Weinberger, "To the Point: 'Understanding Music's Emotional Powers,'" *MuSICA Research Notes*, *2001*, Volume VIII, Issue 1 (Winter 2001). http://www.musica.uci.edu.

CHAPTER FIVE

CHRISTIAN LYRICS CANNOT MAKE WRONG MUSIC RIGHT

When you listen to what I'm playing, you got to see in your mind all them gals out there swinging their [b . . . s] and getting the mens [sic] excited. Otherwise you ain't got this music rightly understood. I could sit there and throw my hands down and make them gals do anything. I told them when to shake it and when to hold it back. That's what this music is for.[1]

Graphic, isn't it? This is a quote from an enlightening article, written from a secular point of view with nothing to prove, which openly, honestly, and without apology, traces the roots of blues, jazz, and rock music. The above excerpt is in reference to a type of rural blues music of the 1930s and 1940s, which was specifically intended for wild dancing.

The music itself was improvisationally played in such a way to evoke sensually suggestive responses in the listeners. The listeners merely acted out the immoral message of the music through their movements because, as previously discussed, the morality of almost any music usually manifests itself in the behavior of those listening to it.

It's interesting that the secular world "gets it" about music and the morality it can convey without lyrics. In a recent music review in the *St. Louis Post-Dispatch* newspaper, the writer referred to a certain musical piece as "slow and erotic,"[2] and for decades, burlesque dancers have been suggestively dancing to equally suggestive music. This type of immoral dance, by definition, requires sensually suggestive music; the dance is just an outward manifestation of the composer's arrangement of the music for its specific intent: a burlesque dance. This type of dance does not match waltz music, classical music, or traditional hymnody.

The great romantic period composer of ballets, Peter Ilyich Tchaikovsky, made the observation that composing is, "a musical confession of the soul, which unburdens itself through sounds just as a lyric poet expresses himself through poetry . . . . As the poet Heine said, 'Where words leave off, music begins.'"[3]

This understanding that the music itself is an expression of the inward man, thus with the ability to convey moods and feelings (one of which is sensuality), apart from any lyrics, is described in a *Time* magazine special issue on music, which explains that when lyrics are indiscernible, it doesn't matter. Listeners can still understand the meaning, because the feeling intended to be conveyed comes through in musical phrasing. One British band selected the words to some of their songs from cut up sheets of lyrics they drew out of a top hat, and an Icelandic band sometimes sings in a made-up language.[4]

This article further discusses the universal ability of our being able to understand the intended message of any music, *even though the lyrics may be in a foreign language.* This is accomplished through the delivery styles and techniques of musicians and vocalists, not through any lyrics.

If you've ever eaten at a Chinese restaurant that plays Chinese pop/rock music, you'll realize this. The music's intent comes through in its style; we don't have to know how to speak Chinese to interpret the meaning of the music. Most likely, the Chinese rock music is secular rock music, similar to our American secular rock with its lyrics about worldliness, rebellion, love, and passion. But it doesn't really matter, because the musical style and vocal delivery convey the message by themselves: we will respond to the music first, the lyrics are secondary.

Text Painting

There's a term in music called *text painting*.[5] It means that the style of the music should match what the words are trying to say. Serious, somber lyrics require serious, somber music. Happy lyrics demand uplifting music.

We saw this concept in chapter one—how appropriate movie music helps to enhance the story line and convey impressions and emotions such as suspense, melancholy, sadness, comedy, optimism, hope, joy, and, yes, sultriness. Joyful music, for example, is never played when the scene is mournful. The idea of text painting is used with great finesse by film composers, although in movies, the music is set to visual images, rather than to lyrics. Secular "pop" composer/artists have an understanding of its importance, too. In fact, it seems that the secular rock musicians understand this quite well: they put angry words with intense, angry sounding music and sensually suggestive words with sensually suggestive vocal styles and music.

Unfortunately, most Christian composers/arrangers and music directors (worship leaders) either don't properly understand text painting to its fullest extent, or choose to ignore it. There's more to applying this technique than adding Christian words to any style of music or playing praise music in an upbeat style and the invitational hymn in a slow tempo.[6]

Much of Christian music today is replete with conflicting messages between the lyrics and the music itself. Our mouths may be praising the Lord and declaring His holiness, but the message conveyed through immoral music techniques far outweighs the message of the lyrics, and we see it manifested in how people react to the music.[7] Words about God's holiness and loose or sensual body movements just do not mix, and as we've seen in the previous two chapters, music influences us more than we realize. [8]

Style matters. Delivery matters. Can you imagine singing the hymn, *Amazing Grace*, to the style of burlesque dance music? See how it doesn't match? Yet, I've heard invitational hymns sung to sensually played music, with sultry vocal delivery.

Lyrics, no matter how spiritual, cannot make sensual music morally pure, because the message of the music does not match the message of the lyrics. Putting Christian lyrics to immoral music doesn't cause the music to become moral any more than attending church makes a person a Christian.

Recall from chapter four the man at the convention worship service, with his eyes closed, swaying sensually to the music. The lyrics were Christian, but the meaning of the music itself outweighed the meaning of the lyrics, as demonstrated by his actions. He was responding to the music, not to the lyrics. Would true Christian lyrics by themselves ever cause a person to sway sensually?

In Christian music, the concept of text painting should be appropriately applied so that both the music and the lyrics demonstrate Christian values and the holiness of God. Reverent lyrics, which show respect and honor to our holy God, should be matched with reverent-style music. Praise lyrics should be paired with uplifting moral music.

Yet, if those same God-honoring lyrics are matched to immoral music, as we saw in the *Amazing Grace* example above, the message becomes a mixed message of sensual Christianity—an oxymoron—which has caused many people, especially men, to stumble morally. Let it be said that traditionally played hymns or other truly moral Christian music rarely, if ever, contribute to moral failings.

These are the possible combinations for music and lyrics:

Moral lyrics with moral music
Moral lyrics with immoral music

Christian lyrics with moral music
Christian lyrics with immoral music

Immoral lyrics with moral music
Immoral lyrics with immoral music

When the combination matches, text painting has been properly utilized and the lyrics have their greatest impact; yet only one combination, Christian lyrics paired with moral music, convey the true message of Christianity. Moral music and lyrics have their place, too, as demonstrated by many wonderful old musicals, such as *The Sound of Music* and *Mary Poppins*.

Notice there is no such thing as "Christian" music. There are only two choices for music: moral and immoral. Adding lyrics that contain Christian theology to music is how we define, or label, music as Christian; however, lyrics don't change the meaning of any musical vehicle. Christian lyrics and sensual music together may send a message, but the musical message far outweighs the lyrical message, as we've seen in the *Time* article. *Christian lyrics cannot make wrong music right.* Immoral music is simply wrong for the moral intent of the Christian lyrics.

Here's the key: Immorality in either the music or the lyrics will corrupt and negatively affect the overall musical piece. Morality matters.

For a musical piece to be truly Christian, we have to apply the principle of text painting fully by using appropriate moral music (a Christian value, anyway) with Christian lyrics. Then, the meaning of the lyrics has more impact and, instead of being side-tracked by sensual music that appeals to our flesh, we are able to concentrate more fully on those lyrics as we apply them to our lives. The moral music is not only sending the same message as the Christian words, it enhances them.

Vocal delivery, that is, the way we sing, also gives a message apart from the lyrics, and apart from the music; this, too, is a form of text painting. Actions speak louder than words, and vocal delivery speaks volumes.

When we speak, people believe our tone, rather than our words. Most of the time, our words match our tone of voice, and we are believable. Other times, we betray our true feelings by our tone of voice and we send a mixed message. The meaning of the tone of our voice far outweighs our words if the tone doesn't match what we are saying. "I love you," gruffly uttered through clenched teeth is far less believable than if it's spoken in a loving tone of voice. This truth parallels and confirms the preceding discussion that when moral lyrics are paired with immoral music, the immoral musical style carries greater weight.

In other words, our tone of voice, not our words, conveys our real message; similarly, the tone, or style, of the music, not the lyrics, conveys the *music's* message.

At my house, once in a while I have to remind my daughters to be "kind" to one another. As soon as I say that, I'll hear one of them sweetly sing their message to the other, and "Quit bothering me," becomes comical, instead of harsh and critical. The tone made all the difference and diffused a situation that could have become unpleasant.

Since people believe the tone of our voice more than the words, it's essential that we are aware of how we sing—our vocal delivery—because if it's done incorrectly, we draw attention to our vocal style, and a conflicting message is sent that overrides the meaning of the lyrics. Usually, that message is a message of sensuality.

In my second book, *Let Those Who Have Ears to Hear*, I discussed Marilyn Monroe's delivery of the song, "Happy Birthday," to President Kennedy. She sang that simple tune in a breathy, whispery, sensually suggestive type of voice, and also changed the actual rhythm of the song to a slow jazz style rhythm, rather than the peppy, straight rhythm it was intended to be. Instead of hearing the words to the tune, people were hearing the "come on" in her voice, and her musical delivery was louder than the lyrics. We can easily observe Marilyn's immoral text painting in both music and vocal style, yet the words themselves were harmless.

There are many ways the voice can be manipulated for various effects, and we'll be looking at these in chapter ten. Unfortunately, immorality in vocal delivery abounds in Christian music today, masquerading as artistry; however, sensuality is not artistry.

For example, trained opera singers never sing in a sensual style, because sensually suggestive vocal delivery is a style that's specifically learned, even by young girls. Yet, very young children don't sing in this manner: they sing honestly and sweetly.

As Christians, we should be very careful that we are not conveying something with our voices that could be considered a "come on" to anyone. We wouldn't do it when we speak to people; why should we do it when we sing?

The secular world understands that musical style and delivery can speak louder than words, and they are truthful about how music affects them. It's time that Christians are truthful, too. And because we are so influenced by music on many different levels, as we've already seen, lyrics don't always matter. In fact, many times lyrics aren't even necessary for certain types of music to arouse feelings and actions that are ungodly, as the quote at the beginning of this chapter illustrates.

I'm well aware that many reading this book will argue that God can use Christian lyrics in people's lives for His glory, whatever the music, and I agree. And although God can use even the wrath of man to praise Him (Ps. 76:10), does this mean that He condones or excuses our sinfulness? Of course not. Therefore, can we honestly think that God *wants* us to praise Him with sensually suggestive music, or apply musical or vocal techniques that are known to arouse immoral feelings and thoughts in others? Would God consider these practices moral?

CHAPTER NOTES

1. Michael Ventura, *Shadow Dancing in the USA* (Los Angeles: Jeremy P. Tarcher, Inc., 1985), 148–149. The quote is by Robert Shaw, a "barrelhouse" piano player (not the noteworthy American choral conductor). A barrelhouse was a small

drinking shack frequented by poor blacks. The musical style called *barrelhouse* is energetic jazz music, usually played by piano, drums, and brasses. NOTE: This book is a collection of secular writings (most of which are offensive) and caution is greatly advised. The chapter, "Hear That Long Snake Moan," is an enlightening, and sometimes shocking, article about the development of jazz and rock music; it should be read with discretion.

2. Sarah Bryan Miller, "Try the Swing 'Bolero' or the Fox-trot 'Bolero,'" *St. Louis Post-Dispatch* (June 24, 2004), sec. F: 7.

3. Joseph Machlis and Kristine Forney, *The Enjoyment of Music*, Eighth Edition, Shorter Version (New York: W. W. Norton and Company, Inc., 1999), 357.

4. Christopher John Farley, "Music Goes Global," *Time* Special Issue (Fall, 2001), 4–7.

5. The concept of text painting, also called *word painting*, was brought to my attention by Alan Ives, music evangelist. See Appendix Four for information about his ministry.

6. There's much more to the art of text painting and musical composition than we need to cover here. Musical composition is not the focus of this book.

7. See chapter ten for more information about specific musical techniques that exhibit immorality.

8. Some people will argue that we are to dance before the Lord, because David danced before the Ark. (David only jumped, skipped, and whirled, fully clothed. 2 Sam. 6:14–23; 1 Chr. 15:25–29.) I discussed this in detail in both of my previous books. Sensually suggestive dance movements, which can and do cause immoral thoughts in others who may be watching,

do not glorify, nor do they honor, a holy God. One should never be more concerned about his or her "right" to dance than about one's personal path toward holy living and exhibiting the fruits of the Spirit, one of which is self-control (Gal. 5:22–24). Also read: *Measuring the Music*, by Dr. John Makujina, Second Edition, pp. 291–301 (Willow Street, PA: Old Paths Publications, 2002); or *Harmony at Home*, by Tim Fisher, pp. 138–148 (Greenville, SC: Sacred Music Services, 1999). See Appendix Four for ordering information.

CHAPTER SIX

THE POWER OF RHYTHM

Rhythm's the key, not drumming, not noise.
Grateful Dead Drummer, Mickey Hart[1]

I was a guest on a call-in radio program a few years ago, and the show host told me about an interesting experience. She had recently attended a percussion ensemble competition. During the competition, the audience remained circumspect as each group played their music. When the last group performed, however, the audience went wild.

Same audience; two different responses. The reason? The final ensemble's music contained excessive syncopation and various other rhythms that appealed to the audience's lower nature, their flesh.

Drum rhythms can be very influential, and because of this, we need to be careful about how we use them in

Christian music; we need to understand their capabilities for good or for evil.

Within the realm of drum rhythms, the military style of drumming is called rudimental drumming, and there are twenty-six basic patterns of drum rhythms that can be executed. These are combined to form the various traditional cadences to which we hear bands march in a parade. In early military units, the drum kept the troops marching, and it's been scientifically proven that certain types of drumming help to keep adrenaline flowing, which was a bonus when the troops needed to rally.

Drummers also sent messages to the troops, such as march, assault, retreat, etc. Even today, the military uses drums for specific purposes, one of which we witness during a funeral procession for a president: the cadence is slow and deliberate, signaling grief and respect.

The rhythm of a march—LEFT, right, LEFT, right—is in all of these rudimental drum patterns. The drumming is controlled, and it keeps the troops in control, much like the previously mentioned audience at the competition.

Drumming that contains excessively accented offbeats, repetitious rhythm patterns, and too much syncopation, however, will create chaos, as demonstrated by the audience's response at the same competition.

The message of the march—rudimental drumming—is a message of obedience, as seen in the military's use of drum rhythms to command the troops. Offbeat rhythms send a message of disobedience, rebellion, and immorality, as we can clearly observe in the audience response at rock concerts.

Rock star Frank Zappa once commented about the power of certain rhythms in an interview in *LIFE* magazine: he asked if one kind of beat only causes foot-tapping, which kind of beat provokes aggressive behavior?[2] He understood that different rhythms cause us to respond in different ways, and we need to acknowledge this fact, too.

Before rock music's inception, western civilization music had always accented the first beat of each measure, with the third beat getting a secondary, smaller accent.[3]

The beat, in this instance, is not a drum beat we can hear, but the natural pulse in music that we use to count the rhythm, and that also causes us to tap our toes.

It works like this: tap your toe (or your finger) four times, giving the first tap a strong accent, and the third tap a lesser strong accent. The effect is, ONE, two, THREE, four. This is counting in four/four time. This type of organized accenting in music changed with the advent of rock music.

Although there had been African inspired musical rhythms brewing in music long before rock music hit the airwaves, such as in blues, swing, and jazz styles of music, when rock music was "officially" developed, its innovators had a specific formula that could be applied to any piece of music: drop the accents from the first and third beats (or counts) in each measure, accent the weak beats, which are the second and fourth beats, and add a drum beat to those same weak beats.[4]

The new rhythm became: one, TWO, three, FOUR. This is the classic backbeat. They purposely did this to inspire teens to, among other things, dance in a new way—uninhibited, with sensually suggestive dance movements. This was rebellion against acceptable moral standards, and they knew it.

The backbeat has many variations, from very subtle to extremely loud; from simple to complex. Yet, in every case, it speaks to our lower, sensual nature, which was its original intent.

We're all familiar with quotes about rock music's beat, such as, ". . . rock music has one appeal only, a barbaric appeal to sexual desire . . .,"[5] and ". . . irrespective of the lyrics of the song, rock music communicates aggressive sexuality."[6] Similar observations have been made by secular musicians, psychologists, and music therapists.[7]

We've also seen in earlier chapters that rock music's beat can cause addiction, release sex hormones, and how, at the far end of the music spectrum, its aggressive sound is sought by rebellious (or troubled) teens. But there is much more to the power of rhythm, and the first phenomenon is called . . .

Entrainment

Have you ever noticed yourself unintentionally walking to the music's beat in a store? That's entrainment. Without our even being aware of it, our bodies entrain to (adjust themselves to match) all kinds of rhythms around us continuously throughout the day; it's easier to go with the flow than against it. Musicians in an orchestra are also entraining together because they're playing the same rhythms, keeping the same musical time.

As defined by composer and sound researcher, Joshua Leeds, in his book, *The Power of Sound*, "Entrainment . . . concerns changing the rate of brain waves, breaths, or heartbeats from one speed to another,"[8] and these internal physiological changes are caused by "an external, periodic rhythm."[9] In other words, our heart and breathing rates, as well as our brain waves, can be purposely slowed or quickened by using music or other steady rhythms that contain the desired target beats per minute, all because of the body's ability to entrain.

Many people find the seashore very calming, with the waves rushing in and out. This is a form of entraining with the rhythmic sound of the waves; after a period of time, our brain waves are soothed into a restful pattern, which in turn affects our breathing and heart rate.

The law of entrainment was discovered around 1665 by Dutch scientist, Christian Huygens. He had put two pendulum clocks next to each other, and soon they had synchronized their rhythms precisely.[10]

Entrainment is a natural and normal part of life and the natural world; however, it can be dangerous if it's purposely misused, as in the case of using New Age music or mindless repetition of a mantra (a one syllable word) to achieve trance, or, in rock music, when *the groove* kicks in.

The Groove

The groove is a rhythmic pattern played over and over until there comes a point in the music (or just a person's drumming) when the drummer "knows" he's "in sync." This groove is very addictive. Mickey Hart, drummer for the Grateful Dead, gives us some insight into its power:

> The backbeat is one kind of drum groove; it's the essential one for rock and roll.[11] I had heard . . . of the phenomenon of rhythmic entrainment that rock and jazz musicians call "the groove." I had even fleetingly experienced it, but Billy taught me to trust in it, to let it draw me in like a tractor beam.[12]

This is the beginning of trance. Mickey also admits that he had to be careful not to let himself go too far into the trance state, because the quality of his drumming would be lost.[13]

The groove, which can lead to trance, is not limited to driving drum beats in hard rock music. Joshua Leeds says, "Repetition with rhythm or *simple melodic phrases* can create a trance state."[14] (Italics added) And trance, or even hypnotism, is easier to achieve than one might think.

Altered Consciousness

Just out of college, I worked at a local cable TV station; our small department produced local television programming. On one of the programs, I filled in for the regular host of a health program, and interviewed a hypnotist to discuss how hypnotism is used in the medical field.[15] The only thing I remember about that program was the man telling me I would be easy to hypnotize. When I asked why, he replied, "Because every time I blink, you blink."

Hypnotists use various means to reach an altered-mind state. But one doesn't have to go to a hypnotist to achieve hypnotism; hypnotism is possible by simply listening to rap or rock music.

Joshua Leeds explains that the even cadence of rap lyrics, together with the steady percussion from a drum machine, actually "slows the nervous system," and "facilitates trance."[16]

In the book, *Are the Kids All Right?* John Fuller discusses hypnotism and how different states of trance are very easy to induce in people, without them even being aware they are hypnotized, because they can continue to be functional and awake. He also informs us that secular rock musicians know very well that they can, and do, produce mass hypnotism by their drum beat alone, and it only takes about one minute to achieve this.

When the audience is in this state, the rock musicians can say anything into the subconscious.[17] This has serious ramifications, and isn't limited to secular rock music.

Several years ago, I talked to a young man who had played in a band at his previous church. He told me that the band was instructed to "work up" the congregation so that they would accept anything the preacher said. Little did they know that this "working up" could very well have been a form of hypnotism, as we saw in the information above, and in my opinion, is not at all ethical or moral. It certainly is a misuse of worship music.

If anyone would know about the power of drums, it's Mickey Hart. He has traveled the globe in search of the "dark" side of drum rhythms, and has personally experimented with these rhythms, and other elements of music, for the purpose of attaining an altered mind-state. He says, "Everywhere you look on the planet people are using drums to alter consciousness."[18]

Alarmingly, this now includes some Christians who have used "Christian" trance music (see Appendix Five) as an aid to entering worship.[19]

But it doesn't end here. Not only are people altering consciousness, non-Christian cultures purposely use specific drum rhythms to call up demons for the sake of demonic possession, mistakenly thinking that this, too, is a form of worship. This is fact; not fiction, not supposition.

Author Michael Ventura writes:

> In Haitian voodoo, as in Africa, the drum is holy. The drummer is seen merely as the servant of the drum . . . through his drum he has great influence on the ceremony. Each *loa* [demon] prefers a fundamentally different rhythm, and the drummer knows them all and all their variations. He can often invoke possession by what he plays . . . .[20]

In other words, by using certain drum rhythms, the drummer is very aware that he can purposely cause demonic possession. This is corroborated by Mickey Hart, from his travels to Africa. He writes, "Particular rhythms are supposed to attract particular spirits. An *Orisha* like Shango [demonic spirit's name] only comes when he hears his rhythm. The most powerful trance rhythms belong to secret societies."[21]

And yet, most Christians still believe music to be amoral, and incorporate into our music similar drum rhythms used in the voodoo religion and other pagan "religions" that practice spirit possession. But is there really any correlation between voodoo rhythms and American rock or jazz music? Consider the following quote by Little Richard, one of the early pioneers of rock and roll:

> My true belief about Rock & Roll . . . is this: I believe this kind of music is demonic . . . . a lot of the beats in music today are taken from voodoo, from the voodoo drums. If you study music in rhythms, like I have, you'll see that is true. I believe that kind of music is driving people from Christ.[22]

West African drummer, Babatunde Olatunji, relates:

> I never became a master drummer in the old sense of knowing all the village rhythms, because when I was twenty-three—in 1950—I won a scholarship to college in Atlanta . . . . when I got to college and first turned on the radio and heard [secular lyrics] I was so stunned. I remember thinking, hey that's African music; it sounds like what's at home. And the same thing happened when I heard gospel music. So I joined the campus jazz combo.[23]

I am not suggesting that all rock or jazz music calls up evil spirits, but I am questioning the practice of Christians using drum rhythms that can be traced directly to those used in pagan worship. Why imitate things that are so completely at the other end of the worship spectrum? Why imitate that which is evil and unholy? God cannot be the author of evil, and neither should we, as His children.

Don't be mistaken; I'm not against the proper use of drums, such as for military style march music, or in an orchestral setting. As I've stated in my other books, (most) drums in and of themselves are not evil; the key is how we make use of them in our music.[24] Rhythms are powerful entities.

At the end of this chapter is a chart, which I believe shows the progressions of worship for both ends of the spiritual spectrum: true worship and pagan worship. True worship seeks to worship a holy God in spirit and in truth, never seeking an "experience," altered consciousness, or to be demonically possessed. Pagan worship, on the other hand, consists of purposely using drum rhythms to achieve trance and/or spirit (demon) possession. Good vs. Evil, exhibited in two very different types of worship.

The drum has played an influential role around the world for centuries. From the European (Christian) culture came military rudimental drumming, as well as a rich musical heritage; from Africa's spirit world came polyrhythmic drumming and other compelling rhythms. Both cultures collided on the shores of America. Once again, Mickey Hart helps us put it all together:

> . . . in North America, the slaves were not allowed to keep their drums and they lost the means by which to keep the rhythms of their spirit world alive. And out of this severing came jazz, the blues, the backbeat, rhythm and blues, rock and roll—some of the most powerful rhythms on the planet.[25]

Chapter Notes

1. Mickey Hart, *Drumming at the Edge of Magic: A Journey into the Spirit of Percussion,* with Jay Stevens (New York: HarperCollins, 1990), 118. NOTE: While Mickey's book is extremely enlightening, it should only be read by mature, scripturally grounded Christians. It contains very serious "dark" spiritual subject matter, and I do not at all recommend it for children, teenagers, new Christians, or anyone interested in the occult.

2. Frank Zappa, "The Oracle Has It All Psyched Out," *LIFE* (June 28, 1968), 91.

3. Rock and roll was white-man's adaptation of rhythm and blues, a primarily black style of music, with its roots coming from African rhythms brought to America by the slaves. When western civilization music is referred to, it means music that developed in Europe, not Africa. (Western civilization music began in the New Testament Church, then spread to, and developed in, Europe. See *Oh, Be Careful Little Ears,* chapters six and seven, for a brief history of Christian music. Chapter three addresses the history of hymns.)

4. Richard Aquila, *That Old Time Rock and Roll: A Chronicle of an Era, 1954–1963* (New York: Schirmer Books, 1989), 5.

5. Allan Bloom, *The Closing of the American Mind* (New York: Simon and Schuster, Inc., 1987), 73.

6. Blanchard, *Pop Goes the Gospel,* 188.

7. See Blanchard, 40–46, and *Harmony at Home,* by Tim Fisher (Greenville, SC: Sacred Music Services, Inc., 1999), 84–87.

8. Leeds, *The Power of Sound,* 37.

9. Ibid., 189.

10. Ibid., 39.

11. Hart, *Drumming at the Edge of Magic*, 185.

12. Ibid., 140. Billy Kreutzmann was another Grateful Dead drummer.

13. Ibid., 176.

14. Leeds, *The Power of Sound*, 155. NOTE: CCM praise music sometimes has repetitive musical and lyrical phrasing, and New Age music has been designed to aid meditation in order to attain trance.

15. It goes without saying that hypnotism is unbiblical and Christians should not participate in this practice.

16. Leeds, *The Power of Sound*, 112.

17. John Fuller, *Are the Kids All Right?* (New York, NY: Times Books, 1981), 137–144.

18. Hart, *Drumming at the Edge of Magic*, 28.

19. Russell Breimeier, "Rhythms of Remembrance," 2001. http://www.christianitytoday.com/music/reviews/2001/rhythmsof remembrance.html.

20. Ventura, *Shadow Dancing in the USA*, 115.

21. Hart, *Drumming at the Edge of Magic*, 204.

22. Charles White, *The Life and Times of Little Richard* (New York: Harmony Books, 1984), 197.

23. Hart, *Drumming at the Edge of Magic*, 215. Note that this would have been rhythm and blues or very early rock music. The gospel music he was referring to was more than likely black gospel; white gospel in the early 1950s would have had straight rhythms with no drums.

24. Mickey Hart relates an account about a Tibetan drum that actually did appear to have a residing evil spirit and how shamans in south-central Russia were given instructions, while in trance, about how to make their drums.

25. Hart, *Drumming at the Edge of Magic*, 210.

KEY TO CHART:
Carnal rhythms are those flesh-appealing rhythms, which originated in Africa and have evolved into American rock rhythms, such as the backbeat and its many variations. Non-carnal rhythms are musical rhythms (melodies), which are played straight, such as traditional hymns and classical music.

My second book, *Let Those Who Have Ears to Hear,* gives a thorough explanation of carnal vs. non-carnal music along with biblical applications.

NOTE: Trance may also be achieved through other forms, as in New Age practices; however, this chart specifically relates to the use of drums for achieving trance and/or spirit possession because these same drum rhythms are found in CCM.

PROGRESSIONS OF WORSHIP

IN RESPONSE TO MUSIC

CARNAL RHYTHMS
Offbeat drums and other
sensual music techniques.

NON-CARNAL RHYTHMS
The melody is priority.

flesh-appealing
rhythms

appeals to the
intellectual/spiritual

The carnal music's effect is manifested
through sensually suggestive body movements.

**False Worship/
Pagan Worship**

Eph. 5:19; Col. 3:16: "Spiritual songs"
(Greek: *pneumatikos*–non-carnal)

True Worship
"in spirit and in truth"
(Jn. 4:24)

lewd behaviour
"works of the flesh"
(Gal. 5:19-21)

"fruit of the Spirit/self-control..."
(Gal. 5:22-23)

chaos/mosh pits
(the sensual gone chaotic)

"...bringing into captivity every thought..."
(2 Cor. 10:5)

"entraining"
(The Law of Entrainment)

"the groove"

trance is possible

demonic spirits respond
to certain drum rhythms
and manifest themselves
in bodily possession.

"Beloved, believe not every spirit . . ."
(1 Jn. 4:1)

CHAPTER SEVEN

MUSICAL INTENT AND MANIPULATION

I recently attended an election-year political rally, which was so carefully orchestrated that by the time the main speaker arrived, the crowd had been worked up to a fever-pitch. This was accomplished through louder and louder, increasingly aggressive and energetic rock music.

Rock concert promoters apply this same technique for a similar outcome: The pre-show music starts out softly, and it progressively increases in volume and intensity until, finally, the audience is "ready" for the performer or band. Sometimes, there's even a pre-show or "warm up" band, which does just that, warms up the audience so that there will be sufficient adrenaline and excitement present to greet the main attraction.

All of this is intent; that is, purposely using a prescribed method (or musical technique) to manipulate the audience to reach a desired effect, and it applies not only to event planners, but to composers, bands, musicians, and vocalists. This is an important discussion for our purposes of defining moral and immoral music, because, as Scripture says in Proverbs 23:7, ". . . as he thinketh in his heart, so is he . . . ."

Composers' intentions come across in the music being written—they are writing what they want to convey to listeners, they are writing what they want the audience to experience from the music, and they are writing from their hearts, where intentions begin.

Contemporary Christian music artists' intents, or motivations, for using rock styles of music are varied, but we need to look at the original intent of these styles of music to see exactly what it is we are copying, because it's this original intent of secular rock musicians that continues to be musically portrayed and results in a desired effect on the listeners, regardless of any lyrics. Recall from chapter five that the tone of voice is more important than the words; the tone conveys the message people believe. Similarly, the style of music, not the lyrics, conveys to us the intent of the music, whether or not we are aware of any particular musical intent.

Christians are imitating rock (or jazz) rhythms and styles that have been designed by immoral people with specific intentions and results in mind, and those intentions remain through the use of specific musical techniques, even though we've changed the lyrics. (Changing the lyrics is also how "official" rock music started.)[1]

As discussed previously, the motivation for the development of rock music was more than just a new musical style: it was planned musical rebellion against earlier morals and behavior. Early forms of rock music—rhythm and blues—emphasized "wild singing, suggestive lyrics, and a loud back beat."[2] These musical elements certainly don't indicate a desire to live a godly life, do they? The intentions of this music are out in the open, and they are immoral.

There are also musically expressed intentions for different types of music. For example, punk rock music's purpose was to deliberately shock people, using aggressive and loud music, with a driving beat, all of which accompanied offensive behavior. *Ska*, another style of rock music, contains compelling rhythms that encourage immoral dancing. (See Appendix Five.)

Contrast these to the music of J. S. Bach, whose purpose for composing was to glorify God and refresh the soul of man, creating musical works that were designed to accomplish these goals. Moral men such as Bach, Mozart, Beethoven, or Vivaldi never, ever, sought to musically influence people towards immoral behavior and it is apparent in their music.

In any music, moral or immoral, the music not only expresses intent, it invites the listener to participate in the morality it is musically exhibiting.

Immoral intentions of composers, and the musicians who play their music, are also revealed by the desire to negatively manipulate their audience through their choice of musical techniques:

Rock star Bob Dylan: "If I told you what our music is really about we'd probably all get arrested."[3]

. . . performers of violent contemporary music do believe that their music has an effect on their listeners . . . they do not perform such music out of the belief that it is harmless, but out of a deliberate desire which in former days would only have been called evil.[4]

By using hard rock, "If a superstar wanted mayhem, he got it."[5]

. . . Jim Morrison (from the rock band, The Doors) intentionally set out to produce the Chicago riot in the summer of 1968.[6]

Concerning the ability to produce trance in the audience, Jimi Hendrix stated, "I always like to take people on trips."[7]

". . . by carefully controlling the sequence of rhythms" any rock group can create audience hysteria consciously and deliberately. "We know how to do it," he said. "Anybody knows how to do it." John Phillips, from the Mamas and the Papas.[8]

Even these rock musicians from an earlier era knew what they were up to musically, and it wasn't moral. It's not likely that the secular world's morals have improved from then until now; in fact, it appears that society's morals have continued to decline generally as well as musically.

I doubt if most Christians would say that their intent, or motivation, for using rock music is to promote mass hysteria or other negative influences in an audience; however, it's alarming that such powerful music techniques are considered amoral and approved for evangelism or worship by putting a few Christian words to these same styles.

If we are copying the very musical techniques secular musicians use to stir up passions, create trance, and cause mass hysteria, aren't those same intended effects inherent in the musical styles themselves, no matter the words? For example, as we've seen earlier in the discussion about text painting, if we matched lewd lyrics to burlesque music, it would have its desired effect. But if we put Christian lyrics to the burlesque music, the music's meaning didn't change, did it? And what about the intent of tribal drum rhythms purposely used for calling up demonic spirits; can we change the rhythms' meanings by simply adding Christian words? No.

With any type of immoral secular music, rock, jazz, blues, etc., it doesn't matter if Christian lyrics (or hymn melodies) are put to these different styles, each type of music's original intent is still musically there due to the specific techniques created to convey those immoral intentions.

In other words, the music's original intent for immorality (or trance, or hysteria) remains in the musical techniques, and again, we only have to look at the behavior of the listeners to see the morality of the music demonstrated.

As Christian composers, performers, and worship leaders, we need to be acutely aware of how we are musically encouraging the audience or congregation to respond. We can even use music—moral or immoral—in a manipulatory manner, such as musically creating an environment purposely designed to move people's emotions in order to gain "decisions" for the Lord.[9]

We have a great responsibility in our use of music, and our intentions should always be to honor God and encourage moral behavior in the lives of our listeners, saved or unsaved. Would God ever want us to encourage immoral behavior or thoughts?

There is an additional element of musical intent, and it has to do with performance.

Intent of the composer comes out in the musical style; intent of the performer comes out in the presentation, which reveals a person's true motivation for performing—self-glory or for the glory of God.

It is no secret that the secular world craves adulation and praise, and if we are honest with ourselves, we as

Christians do, too. It's an unfortunate fact of our sin-nature (that needs to be rooted out of our lives).

Far too many times, Christian vocalists and musicians adopt worldly performance styles that only bring attention and praise to themselves, robbing God of His due glory. Of course it is never wrong to do our best for the Lord, to be accomplished in any endeavor. Yet we cross the line into worldliness by imitating secular performance styles that come across as too polished, sensually suggestive, or staged, such as closing the eyes; facial expressions that run the gamut from sensual to angry; swaying side to side or outright suggestive dancing; holding the microphone close to the mouth and laying the head over to one side; staring into another performer's eyes while singing; jumping all around, and other stage antics copied straight from a secular rock concert; and vocal stylings which present more of a "come on" than honest humility. To be like the world's sensual entertainment, to perform as if we are a famous performer or rock star, should not be a Christian's intent; however, that is the message we are sending in contemporary Christian music.

Whatever our intentions, musically or through performance, they will be perceived by the audience, and the audience will react accordingly. We are always musically influencing, musically manipulating, our listeners for either good or evil. Therefore, we need to check our intent, our motivation, for what we are doing in these areas, and if our intent is perceived by our listeners as something other than to honestly glorify the Lord and help people focus on Him, then we need to change the music, our presentation, or both.

I would hope that no sincere Christian artist would want to imitate the rebellious and corrupt musical styles and morals of ungodly men and women, or manipulate an audience in the negative ways we've seen in this chapter. But we seriously need to consider just what it is we are actually accomplishing with our Christian music.

What is our own personal motivation for the music we choose? If we are composers, musicians, or performers, why does the audience react the way it does to our music? Are we musically influencing our listeners, or ourselves, toward godliness or ungodliness? Are we encouraging little girls towards sensual behavior through our performance style? And which original musical intentions are we imitating, moral or immoral?

CHAPTER NOTES

1. This is documented in almost any book that honestly tells about the history of rock and roll music. Lewd and suggestive rhythm and blues lyrics were cleaned up, the wild rhythms were tamed, and new songs (called cover versions) were recorded by white artists. See Richard Aquila, *That Old Time Rock and Roll: A Chronicle of an Era, 1954–1963* (New York: Shirmer Books, 1989), 7.

2. From *That Old Time Rock and Roll*, by Richard Aquila, 3, Schirmer Books, © 1989, Shirmer Books. Reprinted by permission of The Gale Group.

3. Ventura, 159. A quote from an interview with Bob Dylan as early as 1965, when the rhythms were mild by today's desensitized standards.

4. Tame, *The Secret Power of Music*, 152.

5. Fuller, *Are the Kids All Right?* 137.

6. Ibid., 138.

7. Ibid., 138.

8. Tame, *The Secret Power of Music*, 153.

9. While it's an important part of worship to provide a (moral) musical opportunity with selected lyrics for people to collectively affirm their faith, praise God, confess sin, or accept Christ, we must take care not to be manipulatory in any manner, as in purposely creating extended musical "moods."

CHAPTER EIGHT

CONSEQUENCES OF USING IMMORAL MUSIC IN THE CHURCH

Let us not therefore judge one another any more: but judge this rather, that no man put a stumbling block or an occasion to fall in his brother's way.

Romans 14:13

It is a sad and sobering thing to hear testimonies from people who attribute their moral failings, or even lack of true salvation, to CCM. Some will say that it was not the CCM that affected these people, it must have been something else; however, can we really and honestly tell these people that it was not? They know their own lives better than we do; they know how the Holy Spirit has moved to convict their hearts. We do not.

In 1990, a booklet was published documenting the testimonies of forty-four young people between the ages of fifteen and twenty-three, who had been negatively affected by contemporary Christian music.[1]

Time after time, these individuals spoke about becoming "numb" or desensitized to the music, becoming addicted to the beat, having a lack of inner peace, and experiencing immoral thoughts with both CCM and secular rock music.

I recently spoke with a biblical counselor who told me that he very commonly sees teenagers in rebellion who first listened to CCM, against their parent's approval, then graduated to heavier rock music because the CCM didn't satisfy them. That may not seem to prove that CCM is harmful; however, it is a shame that CCM is used as a tool of rebellion against parents. And it further signifies that contemporary Christian music acts as both conduit and catalyst to arouse the musical appetites for increasingly vile and immoral music. Many of the above forty-four testimonies also mentioned this fact.

The counselor also related the following:

> I recently had a counselee with a severe sexual addiction. He could not overcome it. He said the trigger for his failure was listening to contemporary Christian music. Whether in church or in the car, this music would stir a strong desire to fulfill the lust. If he was to walk in freedom, he had to put it out of his life.[2]

This is not an unusual circumstance, and I would say immoral thoughts, triggered by the sensual sound and delivery techniques of CCM, are common in our churches. For example, I was told about a church worship service that regularly incorporated "interpretive dancing" during which women performed to contemporary Christian music. Although these women were dressed modestly in long, loose robes, the movements they made were so sensually suggestive that many men were having trouble with immoral thoughts. These men, as a group, told the pastor to either stop the dancing or they would have to leave the church. (Recall that the morality of almost any music usually manifests itself in behavior, such as seen here with sensual dancing.)

We have enough troubles trying to stay the course in our Christian lives, why add the negative influence of immoral music, Christian or otherwise? And why promote such music in church where we go to seek refuge from the world and its temptations, as well as for spiritual edification? *Why are we contributing to people's moral failures within the Church?*

A young man from Texas sent me his testimony concerning his earlier participation in a church youth group. Although the church, itself, held to conservative doctrine and values, the youth group activities regularly included contemporary Christian music. He wrote:

> After time . . . I noticed something disturbing every time I was at a youth group function: I had severe struggles keeping my thought life pure. My parents also noticed drastic changes in my attitude after coming home from each youth group activity. Rather than being respectful, I was disrespectful and irritable.[3]

He also noted that his family realized these problems were directly related to the contemporary Christian music, even though at that time they had no knowledge of how influential music can be.

We could continue to list testimony after testimony about how CCM has negatively affected people of all ages (and they are out there); however, there would be recurring themes: immoral thought-life or sensual feelings, a desire for a stronger and heavier beat, rebellion against parental standards (for teens), and a progressing from CCM to secular styles of music and way of life.

As we have previously observed, science has shown that music touches our emotions in ways we cannot even begin to understand, and the consequences of listening to any type of sensual contemporary Christian music, to either ourselves or others, far too often result in moral failure and false spirituality. Some even attribute their lack of true salvation directly to CCM, because the adrenaline high or emotional satisfaction it provided was confused with a true and cleansing rebirth that stems from faith alone.

We are told by Jesus in Matthew 18:6, "But whoso shall offend one of these little ones which believe in me, it were better for him that a millstone were hanged about his neck, and that he were drowned in the depth of the sea." *Offend*, in the Greek, has the meaning in this verse of "entice to sin," and certainly in many testimonies, contemporary Christian music, and praise and worship music that contains subtler elements of rock music techniques, have been the enticements to sin, either as a form of rebellion against parents or as a cause of immoral thoughts and/or behavior.

How many people are we going to offend, how many people are we going to actually cause to sin, before we stop using contemporary Christian music? Causing one group of people to sin is not the "price" we must pay in order to evangelize another group of people. We can evangelize without causing spiritual or moral harm.

The fact that CCM (which includes soft rock praise and worship music) not only entices people to sin but actually causes immoral thoughts and behaviors, such as sensual dancing, should be a very sobering realization to those of us who name the name of Jesus Christ as our Savior.

May it also be a wake-up call to those who lead in worship, sing, compose, or otherwise promote any form of contemporary Christian music that contains immoral music techniques.

CHAPTER NOTES

1. "The Unrecognized Enemy in the Church" (Oak Brook, IL: Institute in Basic Life Principles, 1990).

2. All names have been withheld to protect privacy.

3. Name withheld.

CHAPTER NINE

THE DECLINE OF MUSIC THROUGH THE AGES

*This historical timeline was first presented in a music
seminar by Alan Ives, music evangelist.
Used by permission.*

If we take a look at the progression of music throughout
the centuries, it becomes evident that once music became
primarily man-centered, rather than God centered, it began
to degenerate step by step as we head toward the end of time,
reflecting the decline of society's morals, as a whole.

This chapter will give a simplified historical framework
for music, covering just the basic periods and high-points
of biblical and western civilization music. A mini-reference
guide to specific types of music can be found in Appendix
Five.

Music Before Man (in Heaven)

"When the morning stars sang together, and all the sons of God shouted for joy" (Job 38:7), is a direct biblical reference to the angels singing together.

Ezekiel 28:11–19 is about the King of Tyrus, referring to Satan. This account tells of his beauty and wisdom before his rebellion. We're also told that God created Satan with musical ability: ". . . the workmanship of thy tabrets and of thy pipes was prepared in thee in the day that thou was created" (v. 13). Satan's fall is described in Isaiah 14:12–20.

Satan knows a lot about music; and as with everything good God has created, Satan works to pervert it, which we will see as we continue through music's history.

Music Before the Flood (3000 BC)

In the line of Cain, was Jubal, who, ". . . was the father of all such as handle the harp and organ"[1] (Genesis 4:17–21). The lines of Jubal taught people to dance.

Job 21:7–15 tells us that these descendants of Jubal, ". . . send forth their little ones like a flock, and their children dance. They take the timbrel and harp, and rejoice at the sound of the organ." Verse 14: "Therefore they say unto God, Depart from us; for we desire not the knowledge of Thy ways."

Finally, Job 22:15–17 relates that these wicked people were washed away in the flood.

Moses' Music (1500 BC)

We read in Exodus 15:1–22 that Moses exalts God in a song he teaches the children of Israel to sing so that they will remember the history of God's leading and help. In Exodus 32, however, is the golden calf incident. Recall the children of Israel dancing around the idol they had made while Moses was receiving instructions from God.

On the way back to camp, Joshua joins Moses, and we read in v. 17, "And when Joshua heard the noise of the people as they shouted, he said unto Moses, 'There is a noise of war in the camp.' And he [Moses] said: 'It is not the voice of them that shout for mastery [victory], neither is it the voice of them that cry for being overcome [defeat], But the noise of them that sing do I hear.'"

This music and singing was not melodious or beautiful, because Joshua said he heard sounds of war. This music was rebellious and immoral, which was demonstrated by the drunken dancing and idolatrous activities. (The morality of the music manifested itself in the people's behavior.)

David's Music (1000 BC)

The Psalms record many of David's lyrics, and we know he played the harp as well as invented musical instruments.[2] Whenever there was a revival, the kings followed what David had written about God.

Nebuchadnezzar's Music (600 BC)

Daniel 3 gives the account of Nebuchadnezzar's order for the people to fall down and worship the golden idol when they heard "all kinds of music," which was created by many diverse instruments. This music was intended to be used for idolatry, rather than for the praise of God.

Music at the Time of Christ and His Disciples (5 BC–90+AD)

Psalms, hymns, and spiritual songs: Ephesians 5:19 and Colossians 3:16. The early Church sang the Psalms, just as they had in the synagogues.

Hymns are religious odes sung in an exalted style. Jesus and His disciples sang a hymn after their Passover meal, and Paul and Silas sang hymns in the Philippian jail.

Spiritual songs are other songs of testimony, praise, etc., that do not appeal to our lower (sensual) nature by way of music or lyrics.[3]

During this time, there was also secular music connected with dramas, festivals, and competitions; however, early Christians avoided imitating these to help new converts wean themselves from their pagan past.[4]

Western civilization's musical roots can be traced to the New Testament Church.[5]

Monophonic Music and Chant (100–1300 AD)

Monophony means a single, unaccompanied melody. Chants, also called *plainsong*, are a type of monophonic song that have a "mystical" sound; three-fourths of the Gregorian chants are made up of entire Psalm texts or selected verses.

Polyphonic Music (800–1600)

[The Dark Ages and Forced Religion]

Polyphony is two or more melodies sung or played together, and this was the beginning of what is now orchestral music. During the earlier centuries of this period, particularly prior to 1300 AD, the Church dominated the development of music and can be credited with carefully laying the foundations of western civilization classical music.

During the 1100s–1200s, troubadours, traveling poet-musicians/composers from southern France, popularized secular songs which, contrary to biblical morals, praised and exalted physical love.[6]

Music during this time doesn't really stand out as great. There were various schools for music around Europe (approximately 1300–1600 AD); however, all musicians trained under the same few teachers. Additionally, the music masters and musicians were unlearned in the Bible.

Renaissance Music (1450–1600)

The Renaissance was a time of new thinking, and now Europe was singing. Previous polyphonic vocal works were simplified and published as instrumental dance music; this helped move along the development of instrumental music in western civilization.

Historically, the focus was now on the study of humanity, rather than the study of God. A shift began to occur from faith in God without question, to faith in reason and scientific thought. Humanism was born.

Martin Luther's German Bible Is Published (1535)
[A High Point in the Reformation]

Martin Luther was also quite a musician and composer, and he's considered the father of Protestant music in Germany. He wrote four-part hymns, called *chorales*, because he wanted the congregation to take part in worship and sing the Word of God, instead of just listen to the clergy sing.

Baroque Music (1600–1750)
- *Directed to God and to the Spirit of Man*

This was a great period of Protestant music, with composers thoroughly acquainted with Scripture. Highly ornamented and intellectual, this music has stood the test of time. The notable composers of this period— J. S. Bach, Vivaldi, and Handel—were all devoted Christian men.

Bach stated, "The aim and final reason for all music should be nothing else but the Glory of God and the refreshment of the spirit."[7] Vivaldi was known to recite Psalms and pray while walking the halls of the girl's conservatory where he taught and composed music;[8] Handel is best remembered for his *Messiah*, although he also wrote other wonderful compositions.

THE KING JAMES BIBLE IS PUBLISHED (1611)

Classical Music (1750–1820)
- *Directed to God and to the Spirit of Man*

This is virtuous, moral music as a general whole, and it was written by all composers to this end, even if their personal life was not exemplary. Music was orderly and balanced, which made it sound organized to the listener. From this period we receive the wonderful music of Wolfgang Amadeus Mozart. Franz Joseph Haydn also composed during this time, with Beethoven composing towards the end of the classical period and into the beginning of the romantic period.

Romantic Music (1820–1900)
- *Directed to the Soul of Man*

Instruments were improved and refined, and orchestration, writing for an orchestra, became highly artistic, which allowed composers to musically express their own feelings and emotions about life. Music became passionate, with compositions containing extreme contrasts between soft and loud. Emotionally descriptive words, such as *dolce* (sweetly), and *maestoso* (majestic) were added to musical scores to convey the composer's intent for the music.[9] Composers of the romantic period include Chopin, Tchaikovsky, and Johann Strauss.

Modern Music (1850–1950)
[Program Music; Nationalism; Impressionism]
• *Directed to the Mind's Eye*

Program music, also called "descriptive music," was instrumental music written to represent moods, poems, paintings, or scenes from actual events. For example, the play, *A Midsummer Night's Dream,* by Shakespeare, inspired Felix Mendelssohn to write music for it. This is similar to today's music for film and television.[10] Berlioz, Chopin, Debussy, Liszt, and Richard Strauss also included program music among their works.

Nationalism was the practice of integrating national or regional folk songs and dances into music, instilling a spirit of pride among the people. Examples of a few works include Chopin's mazurkas, Dvorak's *Slavonic Dances,* and Liszt's *Hungarian Rhapsodies.*[11]

Impressionism developed in France giving us "impressions" of things, such as in Debussy's *Claire de Lune* (Moonlight) and *La Mer* (The Sea).

Natural Music (1877+)
[Ballets]
• *Directed to the Body of Man*

It was during this time that ballets composed by Tchaikovsky set the standard for ballet music that was to follow. Ballet dancing had been around for centuries; however, it wasn't until the late nineteenth century that choreography became notable, with highly coveted leading roles in ballets such as *Swan Lake, Sleeping Beauty*, and *The Nutcracker.*

Experimental Music (1900+)
[Scientific Music]
- *Directed to the Undisciplined and Unrestrained Sexual Passions of Man*
- *Evolution Has Been Applied Here*

Experimental music follows none of the rules, structures, or styles previously set forth throughout history, and makes no sense, following the idea of "doing what we want, whenever we want to do it." Imagine a group of instrumentalists simultaneously playing whatever sounds or melodies each one wanted during a concert. (Also see Appendix Five.)

The theory of evolution applies to experimental/scientific music because just as evolutionists believe that animals evolved into people, from simple to more complex, and therefore better, secularists believe the arts are getting better and better because we're more "enlightened."

This is contrary to Scripture. It should be very clear to us as Christians that the arts are getting more and more sinful.

Because it breaks all the rules of moral music, experimental music is selfish music.

Popular Music/Animal Music (1900+)
- *Directed to the Undisciplined and Unrestrained Sexual Passions of Man*
- *Evolution Applies*

Influenced by syncopated rhythms from other cultures, particularly rhythms from Africa, music in the U.S. begins to swing (late 1800s). The swing era, the jazz era, rhythm and blues, and rock and roll develop and begin to define American music.

Some of the music and dances of this time had animal names, and America learned such dances as the Jitterbug, the Fox-trot, the Monkey, and the Funky Chicken. This parallels the theory that evolutionists believe humans to be nothing more than educated animals.

Immorality spread and God continued to be pushed out. The message of "do what we want," and "have a good time" prevails.

Satanic Music (1965+)
- *Directed to Worship of Self and the Devil*
- *Humanism*

People have been deceived; Satan has gone from having musical abilities in heaven to getting his desire—perverted, evil music and worship of himself.

While we are the beneficiaries of many beautiful and outstanding innovations in music through the centuries, viewing this historical timeline of music's development and decline through the ages helps us understand that music (and other arts) reflects the morality of mankind. And as evil men wax worse and worse, music's morality also degenerates as people seek to please themselves, rather than God.[12]

Special thank you to Mr. Ives for his permission to share these insights from his seminar on music. See Appendix Four for contact information.

Chapter Notes

1. An organ was a reed (wind) instrument; that is, it was to be blown with the mouth.

2. 1 Chron. 23:5.

3. My second book, *Let Those Who Have Ears to Hear*, gives a thorough explanation and biblical application of the term "spiritual songs," as indicated by the Greek.

4. Donald Jay Grout, *A History of Western Music,* Revised Edition (New York: W.W. Norton and Company, Inc., 1973), 11–12.

5. Ibid., 2.

6. Paul B. Diehl, "Troubadour." *World Book Online Reference Center,* 2004. World Book, Inc. (Nov. 1, 2004). http://www.worldbookonline.com/wb/Article?id=ar568160.

7. Machlis, *The Enjoyment of Music*, 152.

8. Jane Stuart Smith and Betty Carlson, *The Gift of Music: Great Composers and Their Influences,* Revised Edition (Wheaton, IL: Crossway Books, 1987), 32.

9. Machlis, *The Enjoyment of Music*, 271.

10. Ibid., 298–299.

11. Ibid., 305.

12. 2 Tim. 3:13.

Chapter Ten

How to Discern Moral and Immoral Music

My aunt is an artist; she can paint beautiful land-scapes and realistic portraits. One day, as she was visiting my mom and looking at the color of some new wallpaper, she commented, "That has a bit of orchid in it, doesn't it?"

Those of us who are not artists probably could not have even discerned the color orchid, but if we could have, most of us would have called it purple. More discriminating people might have said the color was lavender, or lilac.

Music is much like art; most people know it has melody, harmony, and rhythm just as they know the artist's palette has primary colors of red, blue, and yellow. Musically, some people can discern a key change or a change in rhythm, like some people can discern a certain color of purple, called lilac.

And finally, just like the artist's eye is trained over time to see orchid, we, too, can train ourselves to discern immorality in music. We'll begin by defining the word "sensual."

As discussed in my second book, *Let Those Who Have Ears to Hear*, there has always been a controversy about appropriate music for the Church. Each generation has had its own new music, and this music was a reaction to what was going on morally, socially, and historically. Each generation's music was "contemporary" to that time, and new developments in music have usually been viewed with suspicion. At the crux of the debate has been the centuries-old concern about what constitutes "sensual" music.

The key to all of this is differentiating between music that is sensual in its intellectual sense, and music that is sensual in its physical sense. That is, distinguishing between music which appeals to our mind, meaning our intellect, as opposed to music that appeals to our lower, fleshly self.

For example, we can delight in the stirring "sensual" experiences of hearing a bird's song, or a babbling brook; these are pleasing to the intellect and to our sense of hearing. In contrast, we can be physically aroused in a different, lower "sensual" manner by immoral visual images, such as those found in pornographic material.

When we apply this to music, moral music will appeal to our intellect and to our sense of hearing; immoral music will appeal to our lower physical nature.

Both types of music may create in us the desire to move or dance;[1] however, each type of music will have an entirely different bodily response, and it is this physical, whole-body response that conveys the morality of the music.

For example, we will tap our toes to the melody of moral music, following the music's natural counts of ONE, two, THREE, four; ONE, two, THREE, four; or, ONE, two, three; ONE, two, three. If one is inclined to dance, the torso of the body will remain straight and fairly controlled, as if dancing a traditional European folk dance, a waltz, or a minuet.

Conversely, immoral music will compel us to tap our toes to the backbeat of the drums, instead of the melody (one, TWO, three, FOUR), or to other repetitious syncopated rhythms, even if they occur in the melody.[2] More typically, though, the backbeat or heavy syncopation will create a desire to move (or dance) sensually: the actions will be loose and the torso of the body will move independently. When those physical responses are exaggerated we can easily see that they are sensually suggestive movements, such as shimmying the shoulders and swinging or thrusting out of the hips.

Can you see the difference in the two responses? One response is to the melody; the other response is to a drum beat or heavy syncopation. One bodily response has *moral* connotations; one bodily response has *immoral* connotations. Therefore, it is observable that the morality of almost any music usually manifests itself in the behavior of those listening to it.[3]

Understanding these two different responses to either moral or immoral music is the very beginning of learning how to discern music, and it's not a question of whether a certain instrument is "wrong"—any instrument can be used morally or immorally. It's also not a question of when a piece of music was written. It *is* a question of whether or not the music contains moral or immoral elements.

This is the key: how and why are you reacting to the music you're listening to? Are you reacting to the melody, to a backbeat, or to other heavily accented syncopated rhythms? If you want to move your body, how is it reacting: with moral movements or immoral movements? Almost any music can be tested this way.

But it does not matter if we want to, or are able to, test music this way. In fact, because each of us responds differently, not all immoral music may encourage us to want to move in a sensually suggestive manner. We can still discern immoral music, because there are specific, objectively identifiable techniques that contribute to music's morality. The first important musical element is . . .

RHYTHM[4]

Rhythms have messages; they say something. This is a vital part of the concept of text painting (chapter five) because rhythms match the philosophy they are trying to teach. These rhythms can also be traced to influences and morals of certain periods of history, as we have just seen in chapter nine.[5] All music has rhythm; a melody is a simple rhythm. Some of the basic rhythms are:

A. The March
• *A Message of Obedience*

In a traditional march, the rhythm is ONE, two; ONE, two, inspiring us to march: LEFT, right; LEFT, right, and the drums either play a variation of a rudimental military cadence, or they actually support the melody's rhythm. The accent is on the first beat, the strong beat, of each measure of two counts.

When soldiers march, they step out on their weak foot, showing obedience and submission to their higher authority. Similarly, we, as Christians, are called to be soldiers of the Lord (not dancers), and we have hymns that impart this truth, such as "Onward, Christian Soldiers," and "The Battle Hymn of the Republic."

Many of the hymns in 4/4 time have a march-like rhythm. The march rhythm is a moral rhythm.

B. The Backbeat

• *A Message of Rebellion*

In contrast to the march's message of obedience is the backbeat's message of rebellion against God. The backbeat is a continually accented weak beat, usually the second and fourth counts, and is normally played by a drum, but it can also be played by other rhythm instruments. Nowhere is this more clearly seen than in the backbeat of rock (or jazz) music, and it doesn't matter if it's very soft or very loud.

There are many variations of the backbeat; what's common to all is that they repeatedly accent, or stress, offbeats two and four more than the strong beats one and three, and they are played in addition to any melody. These additional drum beats are what we will react to (instead of the melody) when we hear music that incorporates the backbeat. The backbeat can be emphasized by many different types of percussive devices. It can also be emphasized in the melody, without drums, such as with the guitar or bass guitar, resulting in a swinging "feel" to the music.

We've previously seen that rock music's history shows its planned rebellious design to depart from moral music's first-beat-strong rule and to purposely cause listeners to react in sensual dance movements.[6] The backbeat is an immoral rhythm.[7]

C. The Straight Rhythm

• *A Message of Purity*

"Playing it straight," is musical terminology for music that's played as written, such as most classical music, traditional hymnody, and European folk music. Eighth notes are played evenly, like the fast tick-tock of a clock or beat of a metronome. The word *straight* carries the implied figurative meanings of honesty and integrity, and this corresponds to the Christian's call to the straight path in life, which is a life of moral purity and self-control. With the straight rhythm, we will usually not hear a regular drum beat, unless the music is a traditional march with full band. (See The March, above.) The straight rhythm is a moral rhythm.

D. The Swing Rhythm
- *A Message of Immorality*

A swing rhythm does just that, it swings. "Swing it" is another musical term, meaning that the eighth notes are played unevenly, giving the feeling of da dah, da dah, dah. And, as mentioned above concerning the backbeat, when any instrument emphasizes the offbeats in the melody, the music will swing. The slang definition of a *swinger* is an immoral person committing adultery.

Some types of swing rhythms are found in jazz and boogie-woogie (also called the "dirty" boogie). The term, *boogie*, came from the African word, *mbugi*, which means "devilishly good."[8] Swing rhythms are also found in Swing Band (Big Band) music. The swing rhythm is an immoral rhythm.

E. Teasing Rhythms
- *A Message of Immorality*

Related to swing rhythms, teasing rhythms occur when a note is held just slightly longer than we anticipate it should be held, therefore, "teasing" us. Usually heard in slower jazz music, its connotation of sensually suggestive teasing is immoral.

F. Excessive Syncopation

• *A Message of Uncontrolled Immorality*

Syncopation is simply a musical accent placed on a normally weak beat. When used sparingly and carefully, it makes music interesting and lively, and its correct use will not cause the body to move in sensually suggestive movements. Properly used syncopation demonstrates self-control.

Excessive syncopation, on the other hand, is too many accented weak beats, either by drums or just in the music itself. It suggests lack of self-control, as conveyed through suggestive body movements made to the music's rhythm. A good example of excessive syncopation is ragtime music, especially the ragtime band music of the early 1900s. Excessive syncopation is an immoral rhythm.

G. Repetitious Rhythmical Patterns

• *A Message of Uncontrolled Immorality*

Like excessive syncopation, rhythmical patterns that are repeated over and over appeal to our lower self, and again, we'll respond to the rhythm with sensual movements. Repetitious rhythmical patterns can be played by drums or by a "walking" bass, which is a bass instrument playing a rhythm that "walks" up or down a series of notes, like stair steps. Repetition can also occur in the music itself, such as when a rhythm pattern is continually repeated by a guitar or piano instead of a drum. Boogie-woogie is an example of music that has a repeated rhythmical pattern. These are immoral rhythms.

Let's now apply what we know about rhythm to the excuse that early hymn writers used barroom or secular tunes for hymns. Is there any traditional hymn that contains one or more of the above immoral rhythms? None of which I'm aware; every hymn I've ever sung has followed straight rhythms or march rhythms, never causing anyone to move in a sensually suggestive manner, nor contributing to a person's moral failings.

A historical example of moral lyrics being put to the tune of what was originally a British drinking song, is "The Star-Spangled Banner."[9] With new moral lyrics to match the already moral musical style, it is perfectly acceptable when sung properly; which brings us to another technique that contributes to music's morality:

VOCAL DELIVERY STYLE

The voice is an amazing musical tool. Used correctly, it conveys a message of morality; used incorrectly, it becomes immoral. Here are a few techniques.

A. Straight Singing
• *A Message of Purity*

Like music that is played straight, a straight vocal delivery style demonstrates honesty and purity. It's without pretense or worldly vocal gymnastics, and the voice lands directly on each note as if we were playing a tune on the piano. This is the singing style of a very small child or classically trained opera performer. We don't all have to become opera singers; however, we should sing without pretense or artifice, doing our best as honestly as we can before the Lord. This is a moral style of singing.

B. Breathy Singing

• *A Message of Sensuality*

Breathy singing is not difficult to imagine; it's singing with a breathy quality rather than a pure, strong tone. The connotation here is sensuality; it is an immoral style of singing.

C. Sliding, Scooping, or Singing Below Pitch

• *Messages of Sensuality*

The vocalist will slide the voice down from one note to another, or scoop the voice up from a lower note to a higher note; the slower the slide or scoop, the more sensual the sound. Similar to this is the practice of singing slightly below the proper pitch, often heard in blues or jazz music. These techniques are in contrast to deliberately and squarely landing on the note's pitch; again, as if playing separate piano notes. Sliding, scooping, and below-pitch singing techniques result in very sensually suggestive sounds; because of this, they are immoral. (Sliding and scooping are also instrumental jazz and blues techniques.)

> NOTE: Sliding and scooping should not be confused with the *glissando*, which is an operatic and classical music technique. Because the operatic vocalist or classical musician makes a brief distinction of each note that is passed over, the glissando isn't sensual.

D. Vocal Gravelliness; Cracking, Scratchiness

• *Messages of Gruffness, Toughness, or Sensuality*

These, too, convey sensuality and are usually used in conjunction with other sensual styles of vocal delivery. Although there are a few exceptions, they are rarely used throughout an entire song—they will usually be applied

95

sparingly. Vocal gravelliness is an immoral vocal style, which appeals to our internal, hormonal organs. Similar to gravelliness, a vocalist may also purposely cause the voice to crack or sound scratchy, resulting in a very sensual sound.

E. Showbiz Singing Style
• *A Message of Worldliness*

We've all heard this style of singing: the vocal style is very much showbiz oriented, like at a variety-type show with a famous entertainer. This vocal technique sounds worldly and artificial (like the person is "showing off" his or her voice), and usually contains one or more of these other immoral vocal styles. This style of singing does not convey honesty and purity.

F. Other Worldly and Affected Vocal Techniques

Weeping, wailing (or yelling), and *gnashing of teeth* (gravelliness) styles of singing make us think of the Scripture about people in hell who are doing just that, weeping and wailing. Gravelliness, mentioned previously, can also sound like gnashing of teeth. A *twangy* singing style gives the impression of a "stiff-necked" person, a negative trait according to Scripture. *Sassiness* suggests disrespect. None of these are joyful-sounding styles of singing, which is the kind of singing Scripture encourages us to do.

ADDITIONAL IMMORAL MUSIC TECHNIQUES

A. Sensual Vibrato

Vibrato means rapid vibration of a tone, resulting in the sound fluctuating around the intended pitch. Vocalists and wind and string instrumentalists do this to "fill out" a note that is held for any length of time. Used correctly, vibrato makes the music interesting and beautiful. When the fluctuation is intentionally slowed, it becomes sensual. Like excessive syncopation, excessive (and slow) vibrato is also sensual.

B. Strong, Syncopated Rhythms

These are melodies that are obviously based on a strong, repetitive, offbeat (or highly syncopated) rhythmic pattern, and can be performed by a single instrument, such as a guitar or steel drum, or an entire band. Some examples include calypso or reggae music, and strong jazz or rock music. The music will evoke extremely sensually suggestive body movements.

C. Dominating Drum or Bass Rhythms

We have all had the experience of sitting in traffic hearing (and feeling) the continuous heavy beat of a drum, drum machine, or bass guitar from a nearby car. Such heavy, forceful (driving) rhythms not only dominate the music, they give a physicality to the music, and we feel it in our chest cavity, abdomen, and internal organs. These rhythms do not have to be syncopated or on the backbeat, they can also hit every beat; the key is that they eclipse (or dominate) the melody. These dominating rhythms are overpowering, if not destructive, and are further examples of rhythms that can cause negative entraining or hormone stimulation (chapter six); they also cause sensual body movements.

D. Unresolved Chords; Dissonance; Distortion

Music should have qualities of tension and release, and we can easily hear this in the simple, two measure "Amen."

The first chord (tension) begs to be resolved (released) to the second chord, which gives the hymn its finality. If the first chord never resolved, we would feel that the piece was unfinished. Tension and release take place many times throughout a piece of music and make music interesting, exciting, and vibrant. Chords that never resolve, or remain unresolved for an extended time, however, create continual tension.

Unresolved chords are also called dissonant. In some rock music, however, the dissonance goes way beyond a chord that hasn't resolved and becomes distorted. The noise emitted makes no musical sense and becomes grating to the ears, such as when we hear certain strident electric guitar sounds, which remind us of high-pitched squealing or low pitched growling.

Extensive musical tension and grating dissonance or distortion contribute to a listener's physical tension, rather than provide audible (and physical) rest and relaxation.

E. Loudness

Music can be electronically amplified too much so that it causes pain or permanently damages the ear's ability to hear (a scientifically proven fact). It can also be so loud that it gives the feeling of invading personal space.

A few years ago, I attended a funeral at which pre-recorded, gentle guitar music was played while people arrived. The music itself was wonderful, although it was played so loudly that it made me feel like I needed to step back. It invaded my personal space and was not at all conducive to quiet meditation.

It's usually music with a backbeat, (or other dominating rhythm) that is played too loudly, and at rock music's inception, loudness was another form of rebellion against moral standards.

F. Low Bass/Bass Guitar; Low-pitched Drums

Overly used, low-pitched tones produced by an amplified bass or bass guitar, or a very low-pitched drum, stimulate internal hormonal organs; the resulting sound and effect is sensual. Some people also experience feelings of nausea.

Beyond identifying specific musical techniques, rhythms, vocal delivery styles, and bodily response to different types of music, perhaps the most important thing we can do is to develop our spiritual sensitivity, our spiritual antenna, in the area of music, because some rhythm and vocal techniques are more subtle than others. It may take a while to learn to perceive what is sensual and what is not sensual, but these nuances can be discerned if we're diligent.[10] Additionally, it is more than likely that new immoral musical techniques will be developed as time goes on, and we will need a developed sense of spiritual awareness.

Nevertheless, by identifying the basic techniques that contribute to music's morality or immorality, we can begin to discern between moral and immoral music, regardless of the lyrics, and regardless of culture. Each culture around the globe will have examples of both moral and immoral rhythms and vocal styles. In any culture, the morality of almost any music will usually manifest itself in the behavior of those listening to or performing it.

Music and the art of painting are much the same. A single color in the artist's palette by itself has no meaning, and therefore is considered amoral. A musical note, by itself, is also amoral. But in each art form, colors or notes can be arranged in such a way that the resulting work is moral or immoral, and as Christians, we have the responsibility to apply what we now know about music in a manner that will refresh and encourage people morally, rather than influence and stimulate them in ways that are harmful or immoral.

Thank you, again, to Mr. Alan Ives for his insights about rhythm and vocal delivery style meanings.

CHAPTER NOTES

1. Again, I'm only making a point here about movement and dance; this is not a debate about whether or not a Christian should dance. For further discussion about dance, read my book, *Let Those Who Have Ears to Hear,* pp. 47–50; *Measuring the Music*, Second Edition, by Dr. John Makujina, Appendix B, "David's Dance Before the Lord," pp. 291–303 (Willow Street, PA: Old Paths Publications, 2002); or *Harmony at Home,* by Tim Fisher, pp. 138–148 (Greenville, SC: Sacred Music Services, 1999). See the Resource Guide (Appendix Four).

2. The drum cadence of traditional march music is a moral rhythm, causing us to tap our toes in support of the melody. See point A. The March. NOTE: Some people will argue that tapping the toes to any type of music, moral or immoral, is not an immoral movement at all; of course this is true. This does not take away the immorality of the music itself, which will be portrayed by those who dance to such music. This argument also does not account for specific musical techniques that make music immoral.

3. Moral music and immoral music are defined as non-carnal and carnal music in my second book, *Let Those Who Have Ears to Hear*. This book draws heavily upon Scripture truths and principles as they apply to music. Specifically, Ephesians 5:19 and Colossians 3:16 are direct references that our Christian music should be non-carnal music; that is, non-flesh pleasing (moral) music.

4. Rhythm and vocal delivery style meanings were first presented in a seminar by Alan Ives, music evangelist. Used by permission. See Appendix Four for ministry information.

5. Also see Appendix Five.

6. Suggested reading (with discernment):
   - *That Old Time Rock and Roll: A Chronicle of an Era, 1954–1963*, by Richard Aquila (New York: Schirmer Books, 1989).
   - *Are the Kids All Right? The Rock Generation and Its Hidden Death Wish*, by John Fuller (New York: Times Books, 1981).
   - *Pop Goes the Gospel: Rock in the Church*, Revised Edition, by John Blanchard (England: Evangelical Press 1989, 1991).
   - "The Oracle Has It All Psyched Out," by Frank Zappa. *LIFE* (June 1968): 82–91.
   - *The Legacy of John Lennon: Charming or Harming a Generation?* by David A. Noebel (Nashville, TN: Thomas Nelson, Inc., 1982).
   - *Shadow Dancing in the USA*, by Michael Ventura (Los Angeles: Jeremy P. Tarcher, Inc., 1985). NOTE: Only read the chapter, "Hear That Long Snake Moan," pp. 103–162, which is about the development of jazz and rock music. Some of this chapter is disturbing, so be advised. The remainder of the book is offensive.

7. Again, the term "rock music" includes all genres of rock music, secular or Christian, which evolved, and continue to evolve, from the original classic rock music styles. Today's southern gospel has also made use of backbeats and other musical and vocal techniques listed in this chapter. See Appendix Five for various rock music styles.

8. Ventura, *Shadow Dancing in the USA*, 106. *Mbugi* is from the ancient African language, Ki-Kongon.

9. Valerie Woodring Goertzen. "Star-Spangled Banner." *World Book Online Reference Center,* 2004. World Book, Inc. (Nov. 1, 2004). http://www.worldbookonline.com/wb/Article?id=ar529760.

10. A music fast may be helpful. See Appendix Two. Additionally, Majesty Music provides video resources that include examples of different musical and vocal techniques. See Appendix Four. Also refer to the CD (and Listening Guide) included with this book.

CHAPTER ELEVEN

RELIGION EXTERNALIZED

The best classically trained musicians will tell you that they play what's in their heart. They want to express the emotion of the moral music to the audience, they want it to be beautiful, and they want to hold the audience in the palm of their hand.

If you've ever been to the symphony, or even a classical solo performance, where the audience remained spellbound until the conductor or musician relaxed, the musical effect was successful.

But we have seen throughout this book that secular rock and jazz musicians have their own agenda, and that agenda has not been to the edification of Christians; to the contrary, it has been to musically manipulate audiences into immoral feelings, behavior, and even hysteria.

This is the type of music Christians are imitating, from soft rock praise and worship to trance CCM and beyond: we are musically manipulating our audiences into behavior contrary to Scripture's teaching, yet this has become normal and comfortable, because many people now regularly participate in this music, either in church or by way of personal CDs and concerts.

Just because something is normal, or customary (and comfortable), doesn't make it moral. It's normal to regularly hear or read about abortion, it's normal to see women wearing tight fitting or low cut clothing, and it's normal to hear rock music every day. We may be desensitized to these normal and common occurrences, but they are not moral.

Theologian, professor, and author, Henry R. Van Til, once wrote that "culture is . . . religion externalized."[1] This includes not only the thinking of the day, but the arts.

If we look back through history and the arts, specifically music, recall that Bach, Handel, Vivaldi, and Mozart all wrote music that was morally upright. Of course, like today, no one was perfect in their era, but there was a general morality that prevailed.

Their religion, or Christianity, was conveyed through their music. It was moral music: their religion was externalized through their art form.

While it's encouraging that there are some young church leaders who are returning to traditional and historical forms of worship (and music), the majority of churches today, however, blend right in with the secular music culture, revealing to all the world that we have imitated their immoral rock music styles, sultry vocal delivery, and pagan rhythms in our Christian music.

This is our religion externalized.

In the summer of 2004, I read a *USA Today* article about a new type of "Christianity," where the secular and sacred are purposely combined as a type of ministry, which is designed to appeal to the eighteen to thirty-four-year-old generation. Proponents of this new Christianity promote questionable secular music and magazines, blur the lines between secular and sacred, and are re-thinking how to "do church."[2] They don't want fundamentalists/traditionalists telling them what they can and cannot do, and they don't want to sit still for church.

This, too, is religion externalized; this is trying to make Christianity palatable to society. And this type of Christianity is not in the Bible.[3]

If this type of Christianity is correct (and it's not), then we will have to re-train our missionaries in foreign countries to adopt the unbiblical and immoral cultural customs of their chosen country, such as multiple body tattoos, nakedness, self-mutilation, and music associated with pagan religious ceremonies, all of which are contrary to teachings in the Bible.[4]

Obviously, the above examples are ridiculous; however, why? Aren't we Christians, in our American culture, adopting and imitating the immoral cultural music (and other) customs of our society, which are also contrary to biblical teachings?[5] We are.

How did we get to this point of a "new" Christianity? By allowing immoral music into our churches and wrongly calling it amoral; CCM was, and still is, a blending of immoral secular music techniques and moral or sacred lyrics. And with the approval of these immoral music practices, we've also invited and embraced the morals, thinking, relativity, and worldliness of our culture right into the Church, using what amounts to immoral dance music for worship of a holy God.

Religion externalized. What is in our hearts is now being revealed for all its worldliness, sensuality, and culturally-influenced thinking. Whatever happened to Scripture's admonition in Titus 2:11–12, "For the grace of God that bringeth salvation hath appeared to all men, Teaching us that, denying ungodliness and worldly lusts, we should live soberly, righteously, and godly, in this present world"?

Advocates of contemporary Christian music fail to realize:

- CCM denies the fruit of the Spirit of self-control by musically encouraging people to "loosen up" and do what they feel like physically doing—subtly in church or openly at concerts, some of which promote aggressive behavior.[6]

- CCM does not encourage godly behavior in response to the music, but rather invites ungodly, sensual actions, thinking, and behavior.[7]

- CCM uses the enticement of worldly music as a means for supposed evangelism; however, the Bible tells us that preaching the cross of Jesus Christ is God's chosen method to bring people to salvation,[8] and Paul wrote that he did not use any means of enticement when he preached to unbelievers, so that God's power would be demonstrated instead of man's "wisdom."[9]

- CCM does not distinguish between moral and immoral musical styles, but accepts all music as amoral, thus also obscuring the line between secular and sacred music.[10]

Contemporary Christian music is our Christianity, our religion, externalized. Its beats are the beats of worldly and pagan musical styles, which were purposely utilized as musical rebellion by men who had low to non-existent morals. Contrast this to godly men, such as Bach and Handel, who wrote morally uplifting music, as well as other godly writers of straight-forward hymn tunes that have stood the test of time. Honestly, whose musical example should we follow: godly men or ungodly men?

Ephesians 5:1 tells all Christians to be imitators of God, Who tells us in His Word to sing "spiritual songs," and this applies to Christians of any culture or time in history.[11]

In my first two books, I explained in detail about this instruction to sing "spiritual songs," as found in Ephesians 5:19 and Colossians 3:16. *Spiritual,* in the Greek, means non-carnal; that is, it doesn't seek to please the flesh in any manner, and refers to both lyrics and the music itself.[12] This type of music is moral; there are no sensual backbeats or heavily syncopated rhythms that cause people to move their bodies in any way that could be construed as immoral.

Yet, how would we rate the types of popular music we hear so prevalently today? Wouldn't we say that they are flesh-pleasing? Why, then, are we imitating it?

While we live in a widely diverse American culture and are the recipients of wonderful advancements in medicine and science, we must always be aware of moral and religious philosophies that may be contrary to biblical thinking; we must be careful to discern the morals of our culture.

We cannot just accept everything we encounter as if it does not affect our spiritual lives, or in the case of music, simply attach the label "amoral," and go on about our business. Neither can we "Christianize" everything. Some things we must reject, such as false religious philosophies and pagan musical practices. We must *continually* apply our spiritual discernment to every area of life; unfortunately, up to this point we've made "decisions" about music, instead of being discerning about the ability of music to be either moral or immoral.

Aside from the fact that CCM imitates morally corrupt, and even pagan, musical practices, we need to answer these questions: Is it moral (or Christian) to use types of music that have been scientifically proven to have negative effects on listeners? Is it moral to use music that causes people to stumble in their spiritual walk? Is it moral to take that which is unholy, such as rhythms from voodoo or trance music, and use them to worship a holy God? If God (the Father) cannot be in the presence of sin, can He even hear our immoral, sensually suggestive, unholy music? Can He witness sensually suggestive movements and vocal "come on"? And are these valid methods to musically externalize a true, biblically moral Christian religion?

In the Old Testament book of Amos, chapter five, God reprimands His people for their lack of devotion to Him, their lack of righteousness, and their worship of false gods. He tells them He is aware of their sins and judgment is coming. He even goes so far as to tell them He will not accept their offerings to Him, and in Amos 5:23–24 we read,

> Take thou away from me the noise of thy songs; for I will not hear the melody of thy viols. But let judgment run down as waters, and righteousness as a mighty stream.

Here, we have God choosing not to listen to their music, but rather calling for His judgment and His righteousness to be displayed.

I propose that because in this era we are indwelt by the Holy Spirit, God still prefers *and expects* our righteous behavior as Christians, rather than any type of sensually suggestive music we might offer to Him; after all, isn't our singing to Him a type of musical offering? We would do well to remember, "Grace is not the freedom to sin, but the ability not to." Therefore, to the best of our ability, pure fruit should flow out of the redeemed believer, not fruit that's spotted from the world.

God also wants us to be witnesses to others for His own glory, not ours. The secular world needs us to be a beacon to show them a better way, and that includes music, not only in lyrics, but in styles, because what's true for the secular world also applies to us: the music we listen to conveys to the world that we are moral or immoral, simply by its sound.

Are we as Christians influencing our culture to God's glory, as did some of the great composers from earlier centuries, or are we allowing the world's idea of culture to influence us?

Culture *is* religion externalized, and by looking around at our American culture, it's evident that the mainstream, secular "religion" of this era is sensual and immoral.

Music is not amoral: Science shows us definitively that music does affect us positively or negatively. Scripture shows us that we are to sing non-flesh-pleasing songs and to be separate from the world's vain philosophies, selfishness, and sin. Testimonies give evidence that people are being adversely affected in their spiritual lives by CCM.

Music is one of God's wonderful gifts to us and it is our responsibility to use it morally, so that it both glorifies Him and is beneficial to us. How does your music externalize your religion? May God grant us the grace we need to turn away from immoral musical styles and externalize our religion musically, as well as in other areas of our lives, in a way that is most pleasing to Him.

CHAPTER NOTES

1. Henry R. Van Til. *The Calvinistic Concept of Culture* (Grand Rapids, MI: Baker Academic, 2001), 200.

2. Cathy Lynn Grossman, "A New Generation Spreads the Word," *USA Today* (Thursday, June 24, 2004), Section D: 1–2.

3. 1 Sam. 15:23; Jn. 15:18–19; 1 Cor. 1:17–25; 1 Cor. 2:4; 1 Jn. 2:15–17; 1 Jn. 3:13; 1 Jn. 4:1–6; etc.

4. Lev. 18:6–19; Lev. 19:28; Dan. 3.

5. See my book, *Let Those Who Have Ears to Hear* for biblical teachings and applications about music, and for a specific discussion about the excuse that Paul said "we must be all things to all men." pp. 81–84.

6. Gal. 5:22–25.

7. Ti. 2:11–12.

8. 1 Cor. 1:21.

9. 1 Cor. 2:4–5.

10. Ephesians 5:19 and Colossians 3:16 are biblical teachings for proper Christian music. See *Let Those Who Have Ears to Hear.*

11. The King James says *followers*, but it means *imitators* in the Greek.

12. A song, by definition, implies music.

CHRISTIAN MUSIC COMPARISON CHART

Contemporary Christian *(offbeat or jazz rhythms, etc.)*	Godly Christian *(straight-forward rhythms)*
1. Disorderly. (1 Cor. 14:33)	1. Orderly. (1 Cor. 14:40)
2. Rhythms originated from pagan culture. (Jer. 10:2a; Rom. 8:7)	2. Religious music of Western civilization originated in New Testament church. (Eph. 5:19; Col. 3:16)
3. Appeals to the flesh. (Rom. 8:5a, 8:8)	3. Appeals to the spirit. (Jn. 4:23–24; Rom. 8:6b)
4. Pictures conflict of our spirit with our flesh. (Rom. 7:14–25; Gal. 5:17)	4. Pure; pictures denial of flesh and self-control. (Rom. 8:12–14; Gal. 5:22–25; Ti. 2:11-12)

5. Tickles the ears to draw people to the church. (2 Tim. 4:3)	5. Acknowledges that it is God Who draws people to Christ through the Holy Spirit. (Jn. 6:44)
6. Imitation of the world. (1 Jn. 2:15; Lk. 16:15b)	6. Separateness from the world. (Rom. 12:2; 2 Cor. 6:14–17)
7. Use of sensual techniques. (1 Jn. 2:16)	7. No such techniques used. Morally righteous. (Rom. 13:14; 1 Pet. 1:15–16)
8. Contributes to emotionalism in worship. (Jn. 4:23–24; 1 Cor. 14:33)	8. Encourages true, spirit-filled worship. (Jn. 4:23–24; Phil. 3:3)

THE MUSIC FAST

The music fast is important and very helpful as we begin to train our ears and spirits to hear sensual/immoral elements in music. It will not remove the lure of any type of rock, jazz, or other sensual styles of music we may like, however. As with any temptation, because we still live in our unredeemed bodies, we must make a purposeful decision to not participate in whatever our weakness may be, depending on the Holy Spirit to help us adhere to our resolve.

Remember to ask the Lord to give you spiritual sensitivity, insight, and discernment about music during the fast.

STEPS FOR TAKING A MUSIC FAST

1. *Remove all CCM/rock music from your life.* Also remove any influence of secular rock music as far as possible. If you watch television, have the mute button handy (and use

it). To put it in Bible language, "make not provision for the flesh" (Rom. 13:14).

NOTE: If you are in a public place that plays rock or other sensual music, as soon as possible cleanse your mind with moral music. (See next step.)

2. *Actively listen to classical music, traditional hymns, or other moral music.* Tune your car's radio to your local classical music station.* Keep it there, or buy CDs from trusted resources. (See Appendix Four.) Most Christian radio is not CCM-free, so if you do listen to Bible-teaching programs, turn down the music when the station introduces a new program or during a commercial.

*If the classical station is airing a jazz, swing, or big band program, avoid those, too.

3. *Continue this music fast vigilantly for at least thirty days.*

AFTER THE FAST

When you end your music fast, listen to a praise and worship or CCM song for contrast. Notice several things:

1. *The vocalist's technique.* Is it breathy, gravelly, and/or sliding around the notes? Is it sultry? If you are married, would you want your spouse to be talked to in this tone of voice?

2. *How does the overall music make you want to move?* Are you responding to the melody, or to an additional drum beat? (Drums don't have to be the only indicator here;

strong, or even subtle, excessively syncopated rhythms in a melody can also cause immoral body reactions.)

3. *Do you get a sense of purity, as with traditionally played hymns?* Or does it sound worldly?

4. *Are you aware of a certain pull toward worldliness that this music conveys?*

5. *If you were to stand before holy God face-to-face and sing in this musical style, would your conscience be completely and absolutely clear?*

QUESTIONS TO CONSIDER WHEN BUILDING A MUSIC LIBRARY

NOTE: Be objective when evaluating music; do not let your feelings/emotions decide. We can learn to like new music: familiarity is the key. Since we hear pop/rock constantly, we are familiar with it, and we begin to like it. The same principle applies to moral music: the more we hear it, the more we will become familiar with it and begin to like it.

These questions apply to both sacred and secular music.

1. *Does this music reflect one or more of God's attributes?* His holiness, His righteousness, His purity, His love, His glory, His redemption, His majesty, His peace, His orderliness, His lordship, His joy, His truthfulness, etc.

2. *Does this music fully comply with moral techniques for music?* (Does every area pass scrutiny?)

- Is the melody the priority, with any other rhythms in support and subjection to it (no backbeat or other repetitious rhythm patterns)?
- To what are you reacting, the melody or the drum rhythms? (If it's a march, remember the drum rhythms are ONE, two, ONE, two, and support the melody.)
- How does your body want to react (morally or immorally)?
- Are the rhythms played "straight"? If there is syncopation, is it used properly (without excessiveness, and delivered crisply and cleanly)?
- If there are vocals, are they honest (i.e., without pretense, sensuality, or "showbiz")?

3. *Is this music reverent?* Does it show honor and respect for Who God is? Joyful, lively music can be reverent, because if it follows moral standards, it's honoring and respecting God's Word and His righteousness.

4. *If there are lyrics, are they biblical?* Are they doctrinally sound? If it's a secular piece of music, are the words in harmony with the Christian life? The words should not contradict what it means to be a Christian.

5. *Do you get a sense of "light" in the music?* Is there a sense of pureness?

6. *Could this music be played around God's throne?*

7. *If there is any check in your spirit, heed it.* (When in doubt, don't.)

If there are sensual, worldly, or other immoral elements in any musical piece, we can be certain that these do not reflect God's true character. Neither do these techniques properly represent the Christian life, nor do they show respect for a holy God.

NOTE: Although New Age music seems to fit into the moral category of music, it doesn't. Much of it is designed to be used for meditation (for purposes of attaining trance). The floating, narrow melodies (not much pitch change) of New Age music also carry with them far-Eastern religious philosophies. My first book, *Oh, Be Careful Little Ears*, discusses New Age music and New Age philosophies (pp. 67–70).

Appendix Four

Resources

CONCORD AND HARMONY
MR. ALAN IVES
328 ROSALIA STREET
OSHKOSH, WI 54901–5366
1-920-231-4807

Mr. Ives is available for music ministry, music seminars/ workshops, and preaching. He also offers Christian music CDs, tapes, and books.

DISCOVER CHRISTIAN MUSIC
519 PIEDMONT GOLF COURSE ROAD
PIEDMONT, SC 29672
1-888-414-4326
www.dcmrecordings.com

Discover Christian Music provides a large selection of sacred music.

FREEDOM MINISTRIES
www.FreedomMinistries.org.uk
info@FreedomMinistries.org.uk

This ministry has several books, which evaluate CCM.

IBLP
BOX ONE
OAK BROOK, IL 60522–3001
1-630-323-9610
www.store.iblp.org

The Institute in Basic Life Principles offers a variety of excellent sacred music, as well as other resources for spiritual growth and Christian living.

MAJESTY MUSIC
PO BOX 6524
GREENVILLE, SC 29606
1-800-334-1071
www.majestymusic.com
info@majestymusic.com

Majesty Music has many God-honoring music CDs and choral books, seasonal cantatas, workbooks for congregational accompanists, and children's character building music. They also offer books and videos to help discern Christian music, including *The Language of Music* video seminar, in which Dr. Frank Garlock explains godly standards for music and plays examples of moral and immoral musical styles.

OLD PATHS PUBLICATIONS
1 BITTERSWEET PATH
WILLOW STREET, PA 17584
1-717-464-6963

Publishers of a variety of quality Christian books, including *Measuring the Music*, by Dr. John Makujina, which thoroughly examines CCM.

SACRED MUSIC SERVICES
PO BOX 17072
GREENVILLE, SC 29606
1-800-767-4326
www.smsrecordings.com

Sacred Music Services carries books about Christian music, CDs, videos, and study guides for biblical music suitable for Sunday school or other groups. Tim Fisher's book, *Harmony at Home*, is available here.

DEAN SHOSTAK MUSIC
PO BOX 465
WILLIAMSBURG, VA 23187
1-800-588-3326
www.glassmusic.com

Visit the web site for a listing of available glass armonica CDs, concerts, and other information about glass music.

MUSIC AND SCIENCE RESEARCH
www.musica.uci.edu

The Music and Science Information Computer Archive, located at the University of California, Irvine, is a great resource for scientific research about music.

A MINI-REFERENCE GUIDE TO MUSICAL STYLES AND THEIR ORIGINS

NOTE: This guide is by no means exhaustive; there are many subdivisions in some categories, as well as regional music and ever-evolving forms of music in the U.S. and around the globe. The intention for including this guide is not to stir up desires to seek out and listen to immoral styles of music, but rather to inform because, unfortunately, many, if not all, of the secular rock and jazz music developments are now being used for "Christian" music.

Absolute music (pure music)—music without any associations to paintings, literary works, or other influences, in contrast to *program* or *descriptive music*.

Acid rock—rock music designed to imitate a hallucinatory drug experience, with lots of amplification and different sounds; developed in the late 1960s.

Air—a simple song, melody, or tune.

Allemande (French; *allemanda*, Italian)—various German dances in 2/4 or 3/4 time, in which the partners hold hands; fashionable in France in the 1700s. This style can also be a movement within a baroque music suite.

Alternative rock—the term was coined in the 1980s to define various types of rock music that didn't neatly fit into other mainstream categories; by the mid 1990s, the term was associated with *grunge* by the general public.

Art rock (progressive rock)—rock music that uses more complicated harmonies and a broader structure than mainstream rock music. It sometimes also adapts classical music styles into the rock style; an early 1970s development.

Ballad—today, a ballad is a sentimental or romantic song, or a narrative poem, set to a simply constructed folk song or sentimental-type music. It can also mean sentimentally-styled instrumental music. Originally, it meant a song that was danced and sung simultaneously.

Baroque—a historical period of music roughly between 1600–1750 in Europe. The music is dignified and carefully crafted, with artistic musical ornamentation.

Bebop (bop)—a complex jazz style, with complicated chord progressions and unique rhythms, improvised melodies, dissonance, high-energy drumming, scat singing; harmony changes in slower music are very subtle; late 1940s to early 1950s.

Big Band (swing band)—large bands of the 1930s–1940s, which played jazz music featuring trumpets, trombones, woodwinds (including saxophones) and a rhythm section consisting of piano, drums, guitar, and double bass (the largest and lowest pitched stringed instrument in the violin family).

Bluegrass—quick tempo, finger-picking style of music featuring guitar, mandolin, fiddle, banjo, and bass. The lead is sung in a high-pitched voice, with additional vocal harmonies; it began in the mid-1940s in Kentucky.

Blues—this sad sounding music originated as African-American folk and slave music in the late 1800s. Several types of blues have developed. Early blues were without structure, sung to an acoustic guitar. *City* or *urban blues* are sung with harmonica, electric guitar, bass, and drum accompaniment, and began in Chicago just after World War II. *Rural blues* is another form of blues. Jazz music has its roots in blues.

Boogie-woogie (boogie, dirty boogie)—a jazz/blues style of piano playing in which a repetitious syncopated bass rhythm lays the foundation for a syncopated melody; 1930s.

Bossa Nova—a type of dance music in Brazil that integrates jazz music with the *samba's* rhythm; 1950s–1960s.

Bouree—a lively French dance in 2/4 or 4/4 time; it can also be part of a classical music composition.

Calypso—originating in the British West Indies (Trinidad) among former slaves, its syncopated rhythms were later influenced by American jazz. Lyrics are often of topical or current interest. Calypso may also refer to a style of folk music found in West Africa, South America, and the Caribbean.

Cantata—sacred or secular vocal music that is part of a narrated story or theme; designed for soloists, duets or other small vocal ensembles, and a chorus. Accompanied by instrumentalists.

Cha-Cha (cha-cha-cha)—a Latin American dance to strong, fast-paced syncopated music of the same name.

Chamber music—(classical) music appropriate for a small room or hall, usually played or sung by a small group of only three or four instruments or vocalists (trios or quartets).

Chant—a type of sacred song, originally not harmonized or metered (no grouping of rhythms), with not much change in the melody. Later, chants were adapted to the Psalms, harmonized, and structured by the Anglican church.

Chorale—a German Protestant hymn style, sung in unison, or in four parts, as developed by Martin Luther.

Classical—refers to both the historical period of western civilization music (1750–1820), as well as the broad term given to music that is composed following the early musical foundations of men such as Bach, Mozart, Vivaldi, Beethoven, etc.; "art" music.

Conga—music for the Cuban dance of the same name commonly associated with Carnival festivities of Latin

America; also a type of drum used in Latin American music.

Contemporary Christian music (CCM)—evolved from *Jesus Music* and *southern gospel*; CCM is any form of Christian music that imitates (immoral) secular styles of blues, jazz, rap, rock, or techno music (and their many derivatives). The term also includes any contemporary *praise and worship* music that imitates soft-rock music, or contains other sensual music or vocal techniques.

Cool jazz (cool)—smooth, laid-back (moderate tempo) jazz music, in contrast to the fast-pace of *bebop*. Cool jazz contains full harmonies and incorporates some classical techniques, instruments, and forms into its style; 1950s.

Country (country-western)—developed from rural southern American folk music and includes both rural and cowboy music. Country music consists of the banjo, guitar, and other stringed instruments, as well as vocals. It has expanded to *country rock*, which is country and rock music combined.

Descriptive music—see *program music*.

Disco (from discotheque)—dance music of the 1970s, originally meant for homosexual night clubs. It's characterized by a continuous heavy beat (usually produced by a drum machine).

Dixieland—a type of American jazz music that developed around 1915 and is associated with New Orleans. A Dixieland band usually consists of piano, clarinet, banjo, trumpet, and drums. The style utilizes improvisation and syncopated rhythms.

Electronic music—music produced by electronic tone generators, out of which today's highly diverse synthesizer has developed. Early electronic music consisted of recording electronic tones and amplified sounds and then putting it together to form "music." (A *synthesizer* is an electronic instrument that can produce any pitch, tone, rhythm, scale, or intensity of volume. The electric piano is a type of synthesizer.) Today, genres include *techno*, *trance*, *house*, etc.

Elevator music (muzak)—Muzak was the first company in the U.S. to make and distribute background music for various public places, hence, "elevator music."

Environmental music—primarily recordings of soothing nature sounds such as rain, wind, ocean waves, or sounds of the rain forest. Often associated with New Age practices, yoga, etc. Also refers to New Age or other quiet music combined with sounds from nature.

Ethno-pop (world beat, world music)—refers to the popular forms of third-world ethnic music, as well as the combining of western civilization music with ethnic musical styles or elements from other countries around the world, such as Jamaican-American, etc.

Experimental music—music that experimented outside the boundaries of previous styles and rules of music, such as plucking piano strings or playing the piano with the forearm, or incorporating sounds such as ringing

telephones, etc. Altering instruments, such as by changing their tuning was also done; early 1900s.

Expressionism—developed around 1910, this music reflected
emotions and turmoil of the era and the composer. It
frequently used no key signature and exhibited restless-
ness in the rhythm.

Flamenco—originally from the Andalusian region of Spain,
a type of passionate gypsy dance with hand-clapping
and heel-stamping to fiery, rhythmic music of the same
name.

Folk music (traditional music)—music of the common people
of any particular region or country, which incorporates
their customs and language. Simple music to sing or
play, it's handed down from generation to generation.

Folk rock—a combining of folk music with rock music instruments and techniques.

Fox-trot—originating in the 1920s, a type of ballroom dance
(with music of the same name) in 2/2 or 4/4 time.

Free jazz—a style of jazz that contained free-style improvisation (music composed on the spot) that followed no
predetermined form or harmonic structure; 1960s and
1970s.

Funky jazz—a type of blues, with an earthy, simplistic quality
as a reaction to *bebop* and *cool*; 1950s and 1960s.

Funk—a type of rock music of the late 1960s and 1970s, which consisted of heavy, syncopated rhythms and a bass beat. The music drew from African philosophies.

Fusion (jazz rock)—a style of music in the late 1960s and 1970s that combined jazz improvisation with the amplified instruments and strong beat of rock music.

Gavotte (French; *gavotta*, Italian)—an old French dance in 4/4 time, similar to the *minuet*, but livelier. The term also applies to the music for this dance, which can be part of a classical music suite.

Gigue (French)—music for a type of lively baroque dance (of the same name) in 3/8 or 6/8 time; or, a movement in a baroque suite.

Gospel hymn—a song that shares the gospel message through personal testimony in the style of a traditional hymn, with a chorus. Introduced to a wide audience by D. L. Moody and Ira D. Sankey in the late 1800s.

Gospel music—a religious musical style related to *gospel songs*, with sounds and techniques of contemporary blues and jazz. Styles also include country gospel and gospel rap.

Gospel rock—gospel music with any style of rock beat.

Gospel song (gospel)—a 1900s development of African-American Protestant church music that evolved from spirituals and religious folk songs from slavery times. Gospel was/is influenced by ever-changing secular music styles, and made popular by jazz singers, such as Mahalia Jackson and Aretha Franklin.

Gothic rock (Goth)—although at first considered a subset of *punk* rock, it came into its own movement around 1979. Some bands were very aggressive; some were directed towards the inner-self.

Gregorian Chant (plainsong, plainchant)—Psalms sung unaccompanied within a limited range of notes and without measured rhythm; instituted by Pope Gregory I (c. 540–604) and sometimes still sung in the Roman Catholic Church. There are eight Gregorian scales used for this type of Psalm singing.

Grunge rock (the Seattle Sound)—a rock music development of the early 1990s, which originated in Seattle. An offspring of *heavy metal* and *punk* rock, with strident guitar chords, heavy drumming, and lyrics exhibiting anxiety or a very dismal outlook.

Habanera (Havanaise)—a Cuban dance (and the music for it) from African origins, in slow to moderate 2/4 time with heavy syncopation. Popular in the 1800s.

Hard rock—rock music that is "hard-driving," with between 100–160 drum beats per minute. Usually played in a major key, with distorted guitar sounds.

Heavy metal—a rock style of the 1970s characterized by extremely loud and dissonant (distorted) instrumental solos and a heavy beat. Many times the music is in a minor key, with themes about Satan or sex. There are many subcategories, which include *thrash metal, speed metal, black metal, doom metal, death metal, hair metal, Christian (or white) metal,* etc.

Hip-hop—an offshoot of *rap*, but with more complex rhythms and melodies; hip-hop contains both sung and rapped (recited) lyrics. The rhythms of hip-hop are dance oriented.

Hornpipe—a one person dance of old English origins and the music for it; in lively 3/2 or 4/4 time. It can also be a movement of a baroque suite. Today, a variation is used in traditional Irish dance music.

Hymn—teaches biblical doctrine and praises God in a majestic style; it usually has no chorus. Hymns (religious odes) have been around since New Testament times, although they differed in style from today's western civilization hymn (see *plainsong*).

Impressionism—French music of the late 1800s and early 1900s, which used harmonies and tones designed to give "impressions" of things such as a scene or mood.

Jazz—a generic term that covers many styles of African-American music, such as *blues, ragtime, Dixieland, swing, bebop, cool,* etc. Most jazz music has a beat that "swings," as well as some type of improvisation.

Jazz-rock—see *fusion.*

Jesus Music—a mid-1900s development within the "Jesus Movement," by new Christians who mixed certain

aspects of their youthful lifestyles (rock music) with
elements of Pentecostalism; a forerunner of CCM.

Jig—a lively country dance in 3/8 or 6/8 time originating in
the British Isles; music for the dance or music with the
same rhythm. Called *gigue* in French, the jig remains a
traditional Irish dance form. (A *country dance* is where
partners form two lines and advance and retreat, or
dance down the line and back to their original positions.)

Latin pop/rock (Latino)—forms of pop or rock music using
Latin and African rhythms and percussion instruments,
such as the conga and maracas.

Madrigal—a short, lyric love poem usually sung by three
or more voices harmonizing without instruments; of
Italian origins during the Renaissance era.

Mambo—from the Caribbean, the mambo refers to both a
type of music and its dance. Similar to the *rumba*, the
syncopated rhythm is in 4/4 time, with the third beat
getting an accent; the music has a heavy beat.

March—a military style of music with specifically accented
rhythms originally designed to move a group of people
along at a walking speed; the march is in 2/4, 6/8, or
4/4 time.

Mazurka—a Polish folk dance in 3/4 or 6/8 time, with the accent on the third beat; also, the music for this dance.

Minimal music (minimalist, process music)—music characterized by the repetition of simple melodies, rhythms,

and harmonic patterns with minimal variety; a 1970s development, some minimal music has been labeled *trance music.*

Minuet—a slow and stately French dance, and the music for it, in 3/4 time; popular in the 1600s and 1700s.

Modern Music—the period of western civilization development of music from around 1850–1950.

Mood Music—sets or maintains a "mood," as for a play; also refers to quiet background music used to set an atmosphere, such as in a restaurant. Sometimes called *wallpaper music.*

Motet—a vocal composition for sacred music, sung without accompaniment, but in a *polyphonic* style (two or more melodies sung at the same time). Originally, a secular form of music in the Middle Ages.

Muzak—see *elevator music.*

Nationalism—a movement in music that incorporated ideas from folk music, events, or celebrated heroes of particular countries or regions, such as Russia, Hungary, etc.; late 1800s.

Neoclassicism—a twentieth-century revival of the baroque and classical musical styles from the 1700s and earlier.

Neoromanticism—a 1930s and 1940s revival of the romantic period musical forms and harmonies of the 1800s.

New Age music—a development in the 1980s and 1990s that corresponded to the New Age "religious" movement. The music is simple, contemplative, and restrained, with repetitive melodic patterns designed to aid New Age meditation and emptying of the mind. Usually piano, acoustic guitar, flute, or synthesizer instrumentation.

New Wave—a late 1970s American reaction to *punk* rock, with simpler melodies and refined style.

Nocturne—French for "night piece," it has a dreamy, sentimental quality and is generally written for the piano; originated in the 1800s.

Opera—originally Italian, this is a musical drama, usually sung throughout, with pantomime, instrumentation, and elaborate costumes and set designs.

Operetta—"little opera;" not serious like true opera, but in comedy or parody form, with light music and dialogue.

Oratorio—a lengthy, dramatic musical composition, usually with a religious theme and sung by soloists or a chorus with orchestra or organ accompaniment; there are no costumes, scenery, or actions. It originated during the baroque period.

Plainsong, plainchant—a simple, unaccompanied melody, sung in unison; an early form of sacred vocal music, dating from the first century A.D. Also see *Gregorian chant*.

Polka—originating in Bohemia around 1830, it's a lively peasant dance in 2/4 time; it also refers to the type of music for the dance. The *polka mazurka* was a *mazurka* modified to be more like a polka, yet with the time in 3/4.

Polonaise—a stately Polish dance (and the music for it), in 3/4 time.

Praise and Worship music (P&W)—a genre of CCM, originating within the charismatic movement. Generally softer in style and more devotional in lyrics than CCM; subtle swing or rock rhythms are common, although some P&W is played straight.

Process music—see *minimal music*.

Program music (descriptive music)—instrumental music of 1850–1900, composed to portray paintings or works of literature.

Progressive jazz—similar to *bebop*, yet more elaborate in technique.

Punk rock—a mid-1970s development, originating in England and characterized by aggressiveness and loudness, with driving rhythms. Accompanied by offensive lyrics and behavior.

Quadrille—(French) a type of square dance and music for the dance.

Raga—refers to Eastern Indian musical scales and melodic patterns used for specific purposes during different times of the day. Also, a three part Eastern Indian composition for instruments.

Ragtime—a late 1800s and early 1900s syncopated style of music, considered an early form of jazz, which combined elements of European melodies with African-American rhythms. There were also ragtime dances, either in the form of ballroom dancing, or as rowdier styles of jazz dancing. The "cakewalk" is a ragtime dance.

Rap—urban African-American music, influenced by chanting in Jamaican *reggae* or *dub* music. Developed in the 1970s, but popular by the mid-1980s, it's characterized by recited rhyming lyrics over a rhythm machine accompaniment. If the lyrics are of a social or political nature, there is usually no accompaniment.

Reggae—a popular style of music from Jamaica, influenced by rock music, with heavy bass, offbeat rhythms, and chanted lyrics that reflected Rastafarianism (a religious group that worships Ras Tafari, a former Emperor of Ethiopia); late 1960s. Offshoots include *ragga, dance hall, dub*.

Rhythm and blues (R&B)—an African-American form of music, which developed in the late 1940s and 1950s from blues, jazz, and gospel vocal music. It was the immediate forerunner of rock music. Today's R&B uses very heavy, sensual bass rhythms.

Rock, rock and roll—*rock* is a generic term for the many musical styles that were offshoots of the original (white) rock and roll music of the mid-1950s, characterized by backbeat (offbeat) accents and played by piano (or synthesizer), drums, electric guitar, and electric bass guitar. Early rock music was really *rhythm and blues* cleaned up and made palatable to the parents of the young, white audiences. The term "rock and roll" was an old African-American slang term meaning fornication.

Rockabilly—a combination of country music with a rock beat; a 1950s development, and again popular in the 1970s.

Rock steady—a derivative of *ska*, with less drums, but more vocals and bass rhythms.

Romantic music—the period of western civilization music from about 1820–1900. Composers during this time expressed their feelings through their music.

Rumba—a dance, and its music, originating among the African-Cubans and became popular in the U.S. in the 1930s–1950s. In 4/4 time, its rhythms are syncopated.

Salsa—(Spanish) means "spicy" or "sauce"; another type of music and dance of African-Cuban (Caribbean) origins, with crude and wild rhythms, similar to the *mambo* and *rumba*.

Samba—an African-Brazilian dance, and the music for it, in syncopated and polyrhythmic 2/4 time.

Sarabande (Saraband, Sarabanda)—a stately dance usually in 3/2 time and the style of music for the dance; of Spanish and Oriental origins in the 1600s and 1700s. It also may be a part of a classical suite.

Scat singing—a style of singing in jazz music, which is improvised, nonsensical syllables made to imitate musical instruments.

Serenade—a classical music piece meant to be played or sung in the evening, particularly by a suitor under his intended's window.

Ska—a forerunner of *reggae* originating in Jamaica in the early 1960s. It combines upbeat rhythm and blues backbeat and *mento*, which is Jamaican folk music. The tempo is faster than *reggae*. Ska has been described as compulsive dance music.

Soft rock—contrasted to loud, driving rock and roll, soft rock is quieter and more sophisticated, while retaining the backbeats of original rock music; a late 1960s to mid-1970s development.

Soul music—a form of *rhythm and blues*, blending jazz and gospel vocal music styles; of African-American origins.

Southern gospel—originally a Southern, folk-style of (white) gospel music, such as four-part quartet singing. Much of it has now embraced several forms of the classic rock beat, swing or syncopated rhythms, and/or the "walking" bass, becoming more contemporary and sensual in its sound.

Spiritual—religious song, or folk hymn, originating among the African-American slaves. Hymns include: "Were You There?" and "Go, Tell It on the Mountain."

141

Swing—a type of relaxed, yet upbeat, smooth-sounding jazz music (and dance) popular from the mid-1930s to the mid-1940s in which all four beats get a light accent by a guitar, bass, cymbal, or drum. *Swing* also refers to the musical technique characterized by syncopated rhythms, with the feeling of "da dah, da dah, dah." The swing rhythm technique can be used at any tempo.

Swing band—a large band that plays swing-style music; also see *Big Band*.

Tango—a dance, and the music for it, from Argentina; highly syncopated, yet slow and dramatic. Popular around 1912 in the U.S. and Europe.

Techno (technopop)—electronic, or synthesized, music with a heavy drum machine beat, originating in the mid-1980s. Subgenres include *trance, tech house, rave,* etc.

Third stream jazz—combines elements of classical music with the rhythms and improvisational techniques of jazz. The term was coined in the 1950s.

Trance—a form of electronic dance music (EDM), which developed out of *techno* in the 1990s. Purposely contains hypnotic bass or drum rhythms. Some forms are used with street drugs, yoga, or New Age practices (for meditation/altered consciousness). Subcategories: *Goa, minimalist, progressive, psychedelic*, and *Christian trance*.

Waltz—a dance (and the music) in 3/4 time, either slow to moderate in tempo, popular during the late 1700s through the 1800s, probably originating in Austria. Some composers wrote waltzes solely for listening.

West Coast jazz—a 1950s development, comparable to *cool jazz*. Small ensembles played improvisational counterpoint (two or more melodies played or sung at the same time.)

Work songs—these were rhythmic group songs to help synchronize the African-American slaves as they worked.

World beat, world music—see *ethno-pop*.

NOTE: This mini-reference guide is a compilation of information from the following sources: *The Enjoyment of Music*, by Joseph Machlis and Kristine Forney; *Pocket Manual of Musical Terms*, Theodore Baker, ed.; *The World Book Dictionary*, Clarence L. Barnhart and Robert K. Barnhart, eds.; *I See the Rhythm*, by Toyomi Igus; and the Internet. See the Bibliography for publisher and copyright information.

LISTENING GUIDE TO THE CD

Please note that this CD is for personal instructional
purposes only; discretion is advised.
Broadcast use strictly prohibited.

Because our culture is so saturated with many types of sensual music, we have become musically desensitized, which can make it difficult to identify immoral music techniques, particularly if they are used subtly. A music fast is very helpful in regaining our sensitivity, and I would strongly recommend it; see Appendix Two.

With the exception of the "straight" instrumental and vocal examples, the following musical clips contain some of the basic techniques—building blocks—of immoral music discussed in chapter ten. These same building blocks are common in various forms of CCM: from instrumental to soft rock P&W to techno. By varying any of these techniques, edgier and edgier music will result. (For example, by increasing tempo; changing drum rhythm patterns; using a drum machine instead of actual drums; increasing volume; using extreme distortion, etc.)

Try to listen for each specific technique listed. (Sometimes it's easier to discern the different components by adjusting the treble and bass controls.)

MUSIC EXAMPLES, WITHOUT VOCALS

MORAL RHYTHMS

1. Straight I
- classical
- notes are played evenly
- music is balanced; melody is priority with no distracting backbeats

2. Straight II
- contemporary-classical
- eighth notes are played evenly
- controlled feeling

3. Straight III
- rudimental-style snare drum supports the melody by playing a similar rhythm
- controlled feeling

IMMORAL RHYTHMS

4. The Classic Backbeat I

- in the style of a ballad
- snare drum accenting backbeat counts Two and Four: (one) TWO (three) FOUR
- light cymbal playing: One and Two and Three and Four and

5. The Classic Backbeat II

- uptempo orchestra
- snare drum unnecessarily accenting backbeats Two and Four
- various syncopated bass rhythms

6. Swing Rhythm I

- slow swing style
- scooping clarinet
- teasing rhythms (notes held slightly longer than we anticipate they should be)
- light cymbal playing various subtle syncopated rhythms while accenting backbeats Two and Four
- subtle, repetitious, syncopated bass rhythm: ONE (two) AND THREE (four) AND, which later changes to ONE (two) AND THREE, FOUR

7. Swing Rhythms II and III

- small combo (piano, bass, drum set)
- laid-back, medium tempo
- sophisticated, syncopated brush rhythms accenting backbeats
- repetitious, syncopated bass line

- big band
- up tempo
- accented backbeats with sophisticated cymbal rhythms
- "walking" bass
- boogie-woogie feel

8. Sensual Jazz

- scooping soprano sax
- teasing rhythms
- subtle "click" playing backbeat sequence: (one) AND TWO (three) AND FOUR; (one) AND TWO (three) FOUR (sequence repeats)
- repetitious bass rhythm: ONE (two) THREE (four)

9. Rhythm Dominant I

- driving (continuous) bass and drum beats
- continuous maracas

10. Rhythm Dominant II

- uptempo orchestra
- driving bass and drum beats

11. Rhythm Dominant III

- techno (synthesized sounds)
- erratic heavy drum machine beats
- heavy backbeats
- rapid-fire drumbeat towards end of clip (opiod-inducing 4 beats per second and 8 bps)

12. Distortion

- slightly distorted guitar
- subtle cymbal on backbeats Two and Four
- repetitious bass drum rhythm: AND ONE (two, three, four)

Vocal Examples
Listen for techniques, not the lyrics.

13. Straight Singing

- pure tones, landing squarely on each note
- controlled feeling

14. Sensual Singing I

- scooping up and sliding down the notes
- showy vocal "gymnastics" at end of clip
- loose feeling

15. Sensual Singing II

- breathy
- scooping and sliding
- occasional cracking; slight scratchy sound

BIBLIOGRAPHY

Aquila, Richard. *That Old Time Rock and Roll: A Chronicle of an Era, 1954–1963*. New York: Schirmer Books. A Division of Macmillan, Inc., 1989.

Baker, Theodore, ed. *Pocket Manual of Musical Terms*. Fifth Edition. Revised by Laura Diane Kuhn. New York: Schirmer Books, 1995.

Barnhart, Clarence L., and Robert K Barnhart, eds. *The World Book Dictionary*. Chicago, IL: World Book, Inc., 1989.

Berendt, Joachim-Ernst. *The World Is Sound: Nada Brahma, Music and the Landscape of Consciousness*. Rochester, VT: Destiny Books, 1991; a division of Inner Traditions, Rochester, VT 05767.

————. *The Third Ear: On Listening to the World*. New York: Henry Holt and Company, Inc., 1985. Translation copyright 1988 by Element Books, Ltd.

Blanchard, John. *Pop Goes the Gospel: Rock in the Church*. Revised Edition. Great Britain: Evangelical Press, 1991.

Bloom, Allan. *The Closing of the American Mind*. New York: Simon and Schuster, Inc., 1987.

Breimeier, Russell. "Rhythms of Remembrance." (2001) http://www.christianitytoday.com/music/reviews/2001/rhythmsofremembrance.html.

Busch-Vishniac, Ilene J. "Sound." *World Book Online Reference Center*, 2004. World Book, Inc. (Nov. 1, 2004). http://www.worldbookonline.com/wb/Article?id=ar520640.

Center for Neuroacoustic Research, 1988. http://neuroacoustic.com.

Cooke, Deryck. *The Language of Music*. London: Oxford University Press, 1959.

Diehl, Paul B. "Troubadour." *World Book Online Reference Center*, 2004. World Book, Inc. (Nov. 1, 2004). http://www.worldbookonline.com/wb/Article?id=ar568160.

Elias, Marilyn. "The 'Mozart Effect' is Scaled Back a Few Notes." *USA Today* (Aug. 19, 2003). http://www.usatoday.com/life/2003-08-19-mozart_x.htm.

Farley, Christopher John. "Music Goes Global." *TIME* (Fall 2001): Volume 158 No. 14: 4–7.

Fisher, Tim. *Harmony at Home*. Greenville, SC: Sacred Music Services, Inc., 1999.

Fuller, John G. *Are the Kids All Right?* New York: Times Books, 1981.

Goertzen, Valerie Woodring. "Star-Spangled Banner." *World Book Online Reference Center,* 2004. World Book, Inc. (Nov. 1, 2004). http://worldbookonline.com/wb/Article?id=ar529760.

Grossman, Cathy Lynn. "A New Generation Spreads the Word." *USA Today* (June 24, 2004), sec. D: 1–2.

Grout, Donald Jay. *A History of Western Music*. Revised Edition. New York: W. W. Norton and Company, Inc., 1973.

Haïk-Vantoura, Suzanne. *The Music of the Bible Revealed*. Berkeley, CA: BIBAL Press, 1991.

Hart, Mickey. *Drumming at the Edge of Magic: A Journey into the Spirit of Percussion*. With Jay Stevens. New York: HarperCollins Publishers, 1990.

Igus, Toyomi. *I See the Rhythm*. San Francisco: Children's Book Press, 1998.

Leeds, Joshua. *The Power of Sound: How to Manage Your Personal Soundscape for a Vital, Productive, and Healthy Life*. Rochester, VT: Healing Arts Press, 2001; a division of Inner Traditions, Rochester, VT 05767.

Machlis, Joseph, and Kristine Forney. *The Enjoyment of Music.* Eighth Edition, Shorter Version. New York: W.W. Norton & Company, 1999.

Makujina, John. *Measuring the Music: Another Look at the Contemporary Christian Music Debate.* Second Edition. Willow Street, PA: Old Paths Publications, 2002.

Miller, Sarah Bryan. "Try the swing 'Bolero' or the fox-trot 'Bolero.'" *St. Louis Post-Dispatch* (June 24, 2004), sec. F: 7.

Ostrander, Sheila, and Lynn Schroeder. *Superlearning 2000.* New York: Dell Publishing, 1994.

Read, J. L. "Creative Harmonics." (1997) http://enchanted mind.com/html/science/creative_harmonics.html.

Schreckenberg, Gervasia, and Harvey H. Bird. "Neural Plasticity of *Mus Musculus* in Response to Disharmonic Sound." *Bulletin of the New Jersey Academy of Science*, Vol. 32, No. 2 (Fall 1987).

Smith, Jane Stuart and Betty Carlson. *The Gift of Music: Great Composers and Their Influences.* Revised Edition. Wheaton, IL: Crossway Books, 1987.

Steele, DeWitt and Gregory Parker. *Science of the Physical Creation in Christian Perspective.* Second Edition. Pensacola, FL: A Beka Book, 1996, Pensacola Christian College.

Stevens, Bryna. *Ben Franklin's Glass Armonica.* New York: Dell Publishing, 1983.

Tame, David. *The Secret Power of Music.* Rochester, VT: Destiny Books, 1984; a division of Inner Traditions, Rochester, VT 05767.

"The Unrecognized Enemy in the Church." Oak Brook, IL: Institute in Basic Life Principles (1990).

Tunks, Thomas W. "Harmonics." *World Book Online Reference Center*, 2004. World Book, Inc. (Nov. 1, 2004). http://www.worldbookonline.com/wb/Article?id=ar246500.

Van Til, Henry R. *The Calvinistic Concept of Culture.* Grand Rapids, MI: Baker Academic, 2001.

Ventura, Michael. *Shadow Dancing in the USA.* Los Angeles: Jeremy P. Tarcher, Inc., 1985.

von Rhein, John. "Classical Music: 'Music and the Mind.'" *World Book Encyclopedia Yearbook* (2004).

Weinberger, N. M. "'Elevator Music': More Than It Seems." *MuSICA Research Notes*, 1995, Vol. II, Issue 2 (Fall 1995). http://www.musica.uci.edu.

———. "Music, Development, Aging and the Brain: 'It's Never Too Late for Music.'" *MuSICA Research Notes*, 1996, Vol. III, Issue 1 (Spring 1996).

———. "The Coloring of Life: Music and Mood." *MuSICA Research Notes*, 1996, Vol. III, Issue 1 (Spring 1996).

———. "Matters of Opinion: 'On the Importance of Being Accurate.'" *MuSICA Research Notes*, 1998, Vol. V, Issue 2 (Spring 1998).

———. "The Powers of Music: A Treatment for Epilepsy?" *MuSICA Research Notes, 1998,* Vol. V, Issue 3 (Fall 1998).

———. "Brain Anatomy and Music." *MuSICA Research Notes, 1999,* Vol. VI, Issue 2 (Spring 1999).

———. "Health and Therapies: 'Mozart Enhances Spatial-Temporal Reasoning in a Case of Alzheimer's Disease.'" *MuSICA Research Notes, 1999,* Vol. VI, Issue 2 (Spring 1999).

———. "Music Therapy: 'Music Therapy is an Effective Treatment for Dementia.'" *MuSICA Research Notes, 1999,* Vol. VI, Issue 3 (Fall 1999).

———. "'The Mozart Effect': A Small Part of the Big Picture." *MuSICA Research Notes, 2000,* Vol. VII, Issue 1 (Winter 2000).

———. "To the Point: 'Music "Gets Through" to Autistic Children.'" *MuSICA Research Notes, 2000,* Vol. VII, Issue 2 (Spring 2000).

———. "Student Music Scientists: 'Physiological Response to Music Stimuli, by Johnathan Stocking.'" *MuSICA Research Notes, 2000,* Vol. VII, Issue 2 (Spring 2000).

———. "To the Point: 'Music Improves Vocabulary Development.'" *MuSICA Research Notes, 2000,* Vol. VII, Issue 3 (Fall 2000).

———. "Matters of Opinion: 'Music Research: A Broad View.'" *MuSICA Research Notes, 2000,* Vol. VII, Issue 3 (Fall 2000).

————. "Feel the Music!!" *MuSICA Research Notes, 2001*, Vol. VIII, Issue 1 (Winter, 2001).

————. "To the Point: 'Understanding Music's Emotional Powers.'" *MuSICA Research Notes, 2001*, Vol. VIII, Issue 1 (Winter, 2001).

Western Oregon University. "A Brief History of the Development of the Periodic Table." (1997) Western Oregon University. http://www.wou.edu/las/physci/ch412/per hist.htm.

White, Charles. *The Life and Times of Little Richard*. New York: Harmony Books, 1984.

Wikipedia (Internet Encyclopedia) http://en.wikipedia .org.

Woog, Adam. *The History of Rock and Roll*. San Diego, CA: Lucent Books, 1999.

Zappa, Frank. "The Oracle Has It All Psyched Out." *LIFE* (June 1968): 82–91.

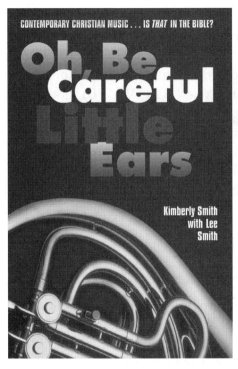

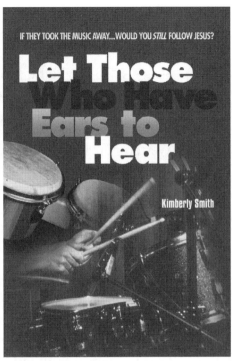

A brief overview of the development of Christian music from both historical and biblical perspectives. Shows why CCM is not biblical. Also includes information about New Age and pop music.

144 pages $9.99

Continues the discussion about CCM—*why* it is a controversial issue and its resulting consequences to the Church. Fifty excuses used to defend CCM are biblically refuted.

216 pages $10.99

1-877-421-READ (7323)

To order additional copies of

Music
and morals
Dispelling the Myth That Music Is Amoral

Have your credit card ready and call

Toll free: (877) 421-READ (7323)

or send $12.99* each plus $5.95 S&H** to

WinePress Publishing
PO Box 428
Enumclaw, WA 98022

or order online at: www.winepressbooks.com

*Washington residents, add 8.4% sales tax

**add $1.50 S&H for each additional book ordered